ALL THE PAINTINGS OF
MANTEGNA
Part 2
VOLUME TWENTY-ONE
in the
Complete Library of World Art

The Complete Library of World Art

ALL THE PAINTINGS

OF MANTEGNA

Part 2

By RENATA CIPRIANI

Translated from the Italian by
PAUL COLACICCHI

OLDBOURNE

London

Printed in Great Britain by
Jarrold and Sons Ltd, Norwich

CONTENTS

MANTEGNA'S PAINTINGS

THE *CAMERA DEGLI SPOSI*

(Plates 80–107)

This cycle is in Mantua Castle, in a square room (805 cm. each side) described in medieval records as the *camera picta*. The name *degli sposi* is not the original name and first occurred in Ridolfi (1648). The frescoes are executed in tempera on the walls. It seems improbable, as Luzio claimed in *Giornale storico della letteratura italiana* (1890), that this decoration was commissioned to celebrate Federico's marriage to Margaret of Bavaria, because Federico is portrayed in the room with two sons and the frescoes do not refer to the marriage. One may more safely assume that if this work was being planned as early as 1471—as indicated, perhaps, by Lodovico Gonzaga's order to provide walnut-oil for the leather hangings of "that room of ours"—the execution began not long before August 1472, when Cardinal Francesco came to Mantua to assume his title of Prelate of the Church of Sant'Andrea. In 1474 the decoration was finished, as inscribed in a tablet held by two cherubs above the door of the Chamber: ILL. LODOVICO II M.M. / PRINCIPI OPTIMO AC / FIDE INVICTISSIMO / ET ILL. BARBARAE EIVS / CONIVGI MVLIERVM GLOR. / INCOMPARABILI / SVVS ANDREAS MANTINIA / PATAVVS OPVS HOC TENVE / AD EORV DECVS ABASOLVIT / ANNO MCCCCLXXIIII. Two of the walls were covered by a heavy curtain of gold leather which continues along the right wall, behind the dais on which the Gonzaga family is gathered. The stones supporting the vaultings rest upon simulated pilasters which give the illusion of a porch running along two of the walls. One of the porches leads to a loggia and the other one overlooks a pleasant landscape, in which the Marquis Lodovico meets his son, Cardinal Francesco. Most critics assess each scene independently from the whole, considering them as episodes in the everyday life of the Court. But E. Tietze-Conrat is probably right in considering the whole decoration as a single unit illustrating the various phases of the meeting.

The ceiling is divided into groins and sections. Those above the corbels are decorated with busts of ancient emperors (see comment on plate 99); at the center the artist painted a circular dome (plate 100) opening out to the sky and framed by a parapet from which sporting cherubs, laughing women, and a peacock look down into the room. Above the frescoes on the walls, lunettes beneath the corbels are decorated with ribbons, vegetable motifs and medallions with mythological symbols (see comments on plates 104–7). E. Tietze-Conrat notes a connection between the ornamentation on the ceiling and L. Laurana's decoration of the gate of the Ducal Palace in Urbino.

Leaking water damaged the

frescoes some time after their execution and as early as 1506 Francesco Mantegna was commissioned to restore them. Further restoration by Martin Knoller in 1790 showed little respect for the original work. D'Arco and Crowe and Cavalcaselle note that Luigi Sabatelli also touched up the frescoes around this time. In 1876 the left wall was carefully restored by Cavenaghi and his work was continued by Gastone Bianchi, Cigoni, and Centenari. In 1941 Mauro Pellicioli cleaned the frescoes and painted over the faded areas with neutral tints. He did his best to try and stop further decay.

Plate 80

LEFT WALL. Mural fresco. General view representing, in three sections, the meeting between the Marquis, accompanied by his children, and his son, Cardinal Francesco Gonzaga, in Bozzolo on August 24, 1472. To the left of the door two grooms are holding a charger and a pack of hounds. In the middle section are two servants with more dogs. The dog on the right is looking up at a group of angels over the door, holding the Latin inscription. The third section represents the actual meeting: on the left, seen in profile, is Lodovico Gonzaga; in the center, facing the viewer, stands the Cardinal; on the extreme right is Federico, Lodovico's eldest son who was shortly afterwards to succeed his father as the third Marquis of the Gonzagas (1478–84). Next to the Prelate and clutching his hand is the "little Bishop" Lodovico, whom E. Tietze-Conrat tentatively identifies with Pico della Mirandola. The young man is shaking hands with the child Sigismondo, who also became a Cardinal. The young profile between the Marquis and the Cardinal Francesco is that of Lodovico's third son,

Gianfrancesco; and the boy in front of him is Federico's son and heir, Francesco, who was to become the fourth Marquis and the husband of Isabella d'Este. The people standing between Cardinal Francesco and his brother Federico are thought to be court painters and, in fact, the face seen on the right between the two profiles might be Mantegna himself. Adolfo Venturi thinks this is a very loose composition, merely a series of portraits. On the other hand, the absolute immobility of each figure and the contrast between them and the elaborate, almost metaphysical landscape against which they are portrayed, are typical of Mantegna's art—always poised between naturalism and stylized heraldry.

In connection with this scene, readers are referred to an excellent essay by Maria Bellonci: "Ritratto di Famiglia," in *Segreti dei Gonzaga*, Milan, 1947.

Plate 81

RIGHT WALL. Tempera. General view of the court of the Gonzagas. Marquis Lodovico II, his wife Barbara of Brandenburg (1444–78), their children and courtiers are gathered together, perhaps waiting for news of Cardinal Francesco's arrival. The Marquis turns to speak to his secretary Marsilio Andreani; next to the Marchioness and holding an apple is probably her youngest child, Paolina (1464); the delicate boy standing just behind her is Lodovico, the "little Bishop," and behind him is the portly Gianfrancesco, Lodovico's third son and future Lord of Viadana and Sabbioneta; standing right behind Barbara is Rodolfo, the fourth son, who was to inherit Canneto, Ostiano and other lands; the young woman on his right is perhaps his sister Barberina, or else Gentilia, the daughter of

76

Carlo Gonzaga, who was brought up with Barberina. The old man between Gianfrancesco and Rodolfo could be the mathematician Bartolomeo Manfredi, or Francesco Prendilacqua, the children's tutor. The family portrait is completed by a female dwarf and other unknown courtiers. The man going down the steps on the right of the pilaster could be Lodovico's eldest son, Federico.

Plate 82
RIGHT WALL. General view.

Plate 83
RIGHT WALL. Detail: heads of Marquis Lodovico and his secretary, Marsilio Andreani.

Plate 84
RIGHT WALL. Detail: Bishop Lodovico and his sister Paolina.

Plate 85
RIGHT WALL. Detail: Marchioness Barbara.

Plate 86
RIGHT WALL. The female dwarf.

Plate 87
RIGHT WALL. Detail: the two figures on the extreme right.

Plate 88
LEFT WALL. General view of the third section: the meeting between Marquis Lodovico and Cardinal Francesco.

Plate 89
LEFT WALL. Detail: Marquis Lodovico and his third son Gianfrancesco, in the third section.

Plate 90
LEFT WALL. Detail: Francesco, Lodovico's eldest son and heir, and his younger brother, Sigismondo, in the third section.

Plate 91
LEFT WALL. Detail: Cardinal Francesco in the third section.

Plate 92
LEFT WALL. Detail: the landscape in the third section.

Color Plate V
THE CAMERA DEGLI SPOSI. Right wall: detail of Barberina, daughter of Marquis Lodovico, or Gentilia di Carlo Gonzaga, with a maid.

Plate 93
LEFT WALL. Detail: busts of the three men on the right of the third section. The central figure could be Mantegna. On his right is the future Marquis Federico.

Plate 94
LEFT WALL. Detail: cherubs holding the Latin inscription above the door in the middle section (see comment on page 75). This part has been restored and repainted several times.

Plate 95
LEFT WALL. Lower part of the middle section: two grooms with hounds.

Plate 96
LEFT WALL. General view of the first section.

Plate 97
LEFT WALL. Detail of the hounds in the first section.

Plate 98
LEFT WALL. Landscape in the first section.

Plate 99
CEILING. General view. At the base of the lozenges beautiful cherubs are depicted holding wreath medallions

with the busts of Roman Emperors, each inscribed with his name: Julius Caesar, Augustus, Tiberius, Claudius, Caligula, Otto, and Nero. The background is decorated with foliage and festoons. Though Mantegna obviously did not execute this part single handed, the decorative invention and the execution, especially the cherubs, are very fine. Some differences from the original paintings are due to their poor state of preservation and to the interference of early restorers.

Plate 100
CEILING. General view of the circular opening.

Plate 101
CEILING. Detail: figures in the circular opening.

Plate 102
CEILING. Medallions with busts of Roman Emperors.

Plate 103
CEILING. Medallions with busts of Roman Emperors.

Plate 104a
CEILING. Detail of a spandrel decorated representing the legend of Orpheus, who is seen here in the underworld, playing his lyre to sooth Cerberus, and to save Eurydice. Both in this and other monochromes in the spandrels one can detect the hand of assistants who merely translated the master's designs into paint.

Plate 104b
CEILING. Detail of a spandrel in which Orpheus is killed by the women of Thrace. In another spandrel, not reproduced in this volume because of its terrible condition, Orpheus is seen playing his lyre.

Plate 105a
CEILING. Detail of a spandrel representing the legend Arion, a celebrated Greek poet and musician of the seventh century B.C. Legend has it that, having been thrown into the sea by some pirates, he was saved and brought back to land by a dolphin enchanted by his music. Another spandrel shows the dolphin carrying Arion on its back.

Plate 105b
CEILING. Detail of a spandrel representing an episode from the life of Periander, tyrant of Corinth (625–585 B.C.), who was called one of the Seven Wise Men of Greece. Shown here is an episode in which two sailors are brought to justice.

Plate 106a
CEILING. Detail of one of the five spandrels decorated with episodes from the legend of Hercules. Here the hero is seen strangling the Lion of Nemea.

Plate 106b
CEILING. Detail of spandrel with Hercules strangling the Giant Antaeus, King of Libya.

Plate 107a
CEILING. Detail of a spandrel portraying the last and most difficult of the twelve labors: Hercules captures Cerberus and carries him to Eurystheus.

Plate 107b
CEILING. Detail of a spandrel representing Hercules with his bow and arrows. Another badly damaged monochrome portrayed Nessus the Centaur with Hercules' wife, Deianira, on his back, being killed by the hero.

Plate 108

JUDITH. *Panel, 30.5 × 18. Washington, D.C., National Gallery of Art.*
Inscribed on the back: AN.MANTEGNA.
A similar picture was listed in a 1492 inventory of the property of Lorenzo the Magnificent. This panel was formerly in the Lord Pembroke Collection at Wilton House, Great Britain, whence it passed into the Karl W. Hamilton Collection, Great Neck, Long Island (U.S.A.), and later the Joseph E. Widener Collection in Elkin Park Philadelphia. According to Abraham Vandardoort a *Judith* attributed to Raphael was the property of King Charles I, who gave it to Lord Pembroke in exchange for a Parmigianino. Some critics believe that the picture reproduced here is that painting. The work was seen at Wilton House by Crowe and Cavalcaselle and by Kristeller, who rejected its attribution to Mantegna (submitted by Waagen) and ascribed it to a follower. Crowe and Cavalcaselle suggested a Flemish artist inspired by engravings of this theme. Mantegna's authorship was at first also ruled out by Berenson. Nowadays the panel is generally accepted as one of Mantegna's masterpieces, though not by E. Tietze-Conrat who believes it to be a development of a general idea originating from Mantegna or his immediate circle. She writes that this is "confirmed by the closely related inventiveness of Zoan Andrea's engravings in the Albertina." Fiocco (1961) assigns it to Mantegna's late period.

Color Plate VI

THE CAMERA DEGLI SPOSI. Ceiling: cherubs in the circular opening.

Plate 109

ST SEBASTIAN. *Canvas, 257 × 142. Paris, Louvre.* From the Church of Notre-Dame, Aigueperse, to which it must have been presented by Chiara Gonzaga who became the wife of Count Gilbert Bourbon Montpensier in 1481. Fiocco and Coletti date it earlier than the *San Zeno Altarpiece* and chronologically close to the *Adoration of the Shepherds* in New York. E. Tietze-Conrat is right in assuming that it was painted at the same time as the *Camera degli Sposi.* A copy by the Paduan School is in London. (See also plates 110 and 111.)

Plate 110

ST SEBASTIAN. Detail: architecture and fragments of sculptures on the lower left.

Plate 111

ST SEBASTIAN. Detail: landscape on the right.

Plate 112

TARQUINIUS AND THE SIBYL. *Canvas, 58 × 48. Cincinnati (Ohio) Art Museum.* From the collection of the Duke of Buccleuch in Paris. According to Landsberger (*Bulletin of Cincinnati Art Museum,* 1953) the subject is probably Mordecai and Esther. The work is a brownish monochrome with golden-yellow lights on a dark brown ground. Kristeller and A. Venturi consider it to be a workshop production. E. Tietze-Conrat believes it derives from an idea by Mantegna, but she is not sure about the execution. All other critics definitely attribute it to Mantegna's last period.

THE TRIUMPHS OF CAESAR

(Plates 113–121)

The nine pictures on canvas (tempera, 274 × 274) are in the Orangerie at Hampton Court Palace. Vasari claims that the cycle was painted for Lodovico Gonzaga, but this is probably untrue for there is no mention of it in records before August 26, 1486, although by that time the work must have been well in hand. We can be sure that Mantegna continued working on the pictures until he went to Rome (1488), when he wrote that he planned to resume work on his return to Mantua. In 1492 he was still painting the series—which in fact was never completed. Some critics think that Mantegna lost interest in antiquity after his visit to Rome, and they base this theory on the fact that his paintings reveal no traces of direct imitation of Roman monuments. But the source of Mantegna's inspiration (as Paribeni rightly observed) was in any case purely literary. It originated (see Giehlow, *Jahrbuch der Kunsthistorischen Sammlungen im Wien*, 1915) from R. Valturio's *De re militari*. On the other hand, I feel that Giehlow's argument—apparently accepted by E. Tietze-Conrat—that Mantegna's ornamental details have a symbolic meaning, is rather far-fetched. References to antique monuments such as bas-reliefs upon the Arch of Titus, Trajan's Column or the Arch of Constantine—these are now in the Palazzo dei Conservatori in Rome—are not decisive. The *Triumph* is a work in which Mantegna's love of antiquity is subject to the broadest treatment: so much so, that it earned him the description, "the Corneille of painting." In its own time, the series immediately caused great interest, although its function seems rather unassuming to us nowadays: the

series, together with another series of *Triumphs* derived from Petrarch, were used as theatrical scenery and casually left outside in all weather. Eventually the paintings were brought back to Mantegna's house in San Sebastiano near Mantua, and they were returned from there to the Ducal Palace at the beginning of the seventeenth century. A short time later, along with the rest of the Gonzaga Collection they were sold to King Charles I who, however, took two years to decide to buy them (1627–9). When in Mantegna's house, the pictures must have been placed between pilasters simulating a porch. This produced an effect of isolating the various episodes and so increasing their grandeur. We do not know whether Rubens saw them arranged in this way or if they had already been returned to the castle when he saw them, but the fact is that he was so impressed that he himself painted a *Triumph*. There are numerous copies of these pictures: in Munich, Siena and in Mantua itself. But the fame of the originals was mainly due to the engravings, especially those done by Andrea Andreani in 1599. Goethe, who expressed his admiration for Mantegna's *Triumphs* in *Ueber Kunst und Altertum*, had only seen the engravings.

Shortly after they arrived in Britain, the pictures were unfortunately restored, or rather repainted, by Laguerre. He ruined the original tempera by covering it with oil and glue. This occurred at the beginning of the eighteenth century. In 1919 Roger Fry suggested further restoration, but what he saw of the work done on the first of the nine canvases led him to abandon the idea. Unsuccessful restoration was carried out between 1931 and 1934 by Kenneth North. Yet, despite so much interference and repainting, Mantegna's powerful structure is still faintly visible.

Fiocco saw a prelude to this series in the polychromes representing *The Justice of Trajan* painted on the front of a chest in the Landesmuseum at Klagenfurt, and which he attributes to Mantegna. But the link between the two works, though acknowledged by Berenson, is not decisively valid.

Plate 113
TRUMPETERS AND STANDARD BEARERS. General view.

Plate 114
TRIUMPHAL CHARIOTS WITH TROPHIES. General view.

Plate 115
THE TRANSPORT OF THE BOOTY. General view.

Plate 116
BEARERS OF BOOTY AND PIPE PLAYERS. General view.

Plate 117
ELEPHANTS AND SACRIFICIAL ANIMALS. General view.

Plate 118
BEARERS OF TROPHIES. General view.

Plate 119
PRISONERS. General view.

Plate 120
MUSICIANS AND STANDARD BEARERS. General view.

Plate 121
CAESAR THE CONQUEROR ON HIS CHARIOT.

Plate 122
THE MADONNA OF THE STONE-CUTTERS. *Panel, 29 × 21.5. Florence, Uffizi.* Also called the *Madonna of the Grotto.* This is undoubtedly the work that Vasari described as belonging to the Medici and which, he claims, Mantegna painted in Rome, therefore in 1488. E. Tietze-Conrat, however, believes it to be one of the *operette* Mantegna sent to Lorenzo de' Medici in 1484, when he wanted the Prince to subsidize his museum-villa. Probably the panel arrived in Florence later, for it is not recorded in the 1492 Medici inventory. Knapp dates it as early as 1466, because the stonecutters in the background remind him of the Carrara marble quarries. Kristeller, on the other hand, is reminded of "a special volcanic formation of basalt" which is peculiar to Monte Bolca, between Vicenza and Verona, and he suggests 1468. He is supported by Fiocco and Paccagnini. In the background of the left wall in the *Camera degli Sposi* are also some stonecutters. F. Hartt thought these were symbols of chastity, related to the Prelates of the Gonzaga family in the *Camera* and, in this painting, to the Virgin. But Hartt's thorough study of Mantegna's complex symbolism does not do justice to the artist's lyricism which is at its greatest in this work. (See also plates 123–125.)

Plate 123
THE MADONNA OF THE STONE-CUTTERS. Detail: head of the Virgin.

Plate 124
THE MADONNA OF THE STONE-CUTTERS. Detail: the quarry on the left.

Color Plate VII

VIRGIN AND CHILD WITH CHERUBIM. Detail of plate 128: the Virgin, Child, and cherubim.

Plate 125

THE MADONNA OF THE STONE-CUTTERS. Detail: the quarry on the right.

Plate 126

MADONNA AND CHILD. *Canvas, 43 × 35. Milan, Poldi Pezzoli Museum.* Former location unknown; sold by G. Morelli to Poldi Pezzoli, a Milanese collector. Restored by Molteni in 1860. The original color is clouded over by yellow varnish which cannot be removed without damaging the delicate tempera underneath. Considered a late work by A. Venturi, E. Tietze-Conrat and Longhi (1962). Knapp and Fiocco assign it to the early Mantua period. Baroni, Dell'Acqua, Russoli, Coletti (who notes a link with Lippi) and Arslan believe it to be an early work. Kristeller dates it before 1452 and Paccagnini at the time of the Vienna *St Sebastian*, that is to say 1458.

Plate 127

THE SAVIOR. *Canvas, 53 × 43. Correggio, Congregazione di Carità.* The marble frame is vertically inscribed on the left side: MOMORDITE VOS METIPSOS ANTE EFFIGIEM VULTUS MEI. Below are other letters only some of which are legible: . . . IA . . . PCS-DD MCCCCLXXXXIII $\frac{D}{V}$ IA. The picture was published by Frizzoni (1916) who interpreted the second part of the inscription as reading: (*Mantin*) *IA Pinxit*, etc. He identified the work—which was then in the Campori Gallery in Modena—with the one sent by Mantegna to Correggio in 1493. This attribution, which seems fairly sound, was confirmed by A. Venturi (1935) and Fiocco.

Plate 128

VIRGIN AND CHILD WITH CHERUBIM. *Panel, 89 × 71. Milan, Brera Gallery.* Acquired in 1809 for the Church of Santa Maria Maggiore in Venice, where it was attributed to Giovanni Bellini. This was a misunderstanding that probably resulted from Francesco Sansovino's *Venezia Descritta* (1604, page 189) in which he described two Madonnas by Giovanni Bellini, together with "a painting of Our Lady, by a most excellent hand." One could hardly identify this work, however, with the one painted for Eleanor of Aragon in 1489 which—as noted by Fiocco, E. Tietze-Conrat and Paccagnini—was to include other figures besides the Virgin and Child. The picture does seem to fit the "painting on wood of Our Lady and the Son with Seraphim" mentioned in the 1493 Ferrara inventory of the d'Este family. The attribution to Bellini survived until 1885 when Cavenaghi restored the panel. Longhi ascribes it to Mantegna's late period and thinks that it has been reduced on each side.

Plate 129

MADONNA AND CHILD WITH THE INFANT ST JOHN AND SAINTS. *Panel, 61.5 × 87. Turin, Galleria Sabauda.* From the Royal Palace at Turin. As stated by Crowe and Cavalcaselle, this cannot be dismissed as a workshop painting but should be considered a very badly preserved work of Mantegna's last years. Recent restoration has eliminated several additions in the upper part and brought to light many repaints. With the exception of Fiocco, most critics agree that it is in fact a late work.

Plate 130

THE DEAD CHRIST. *Canvas, 66 ×
81. Milan, Brera Gallery*. A picture of
the same subject (*Foreshortened Christ*)
is mentioned by Lodovico Mantegna
in a letter (October 2, 1506) as being
among the works left in his father's
study after his death, and has always
been identified with this canvas—
though not by H. Tietze and E.
Tietze-Conrat who claim that *The
Dead Christ* (plate 168) is the one
which they found in the United
States (*Art in America*, 1941). They
are now supported by Fiocco. The
painting that was in Mantegna's
house passed into the possession of
Cardinal Sigismondo Gonzaga. After
the sack of Mantua in 1630, it was
acquired by Cardinal Mazarin, who
kept it first in Rome and later in
France, where it became the property
of Giuseppe Bossi. The Brera Gallery
purchased it from Bossi's heirs in
1824. A similar canvas with the
figures of the mourners was mentioned in the *Journal de voyage du chev.
Bernin en France* (Paris, 1885) as
having been offered by Camillo
Pamphili to the King of France in
1665. Yet another version was
recorded in Naples by Summonte.
E. Tietze-Conrat is wrong in be-
lieving that the heads of the Virgin
and St John are a later insertion.
But the two figures are generally
considered superfluous, although
the composition is very typical of
Mantegna's last period. Kristeller,
Arslan, and Longhi believe Mantegna painted the work when he was
over eighty. (See also plate 131.)

Plate 131

THE DEAD CHRIST. Detail: Mary
and St John.

Plate 132

MADONNA DELLA VITTORIA. *Can-
vas, 280 × 160. Paris, Louvre*. Offered
as an ex voto by Francesco Gonzaga,
after the Battle of Fornovo on July
6, 1495, this altarpiece was erected
a year after the Battle in the Church
of Sant'Andrea in Mantua, under
the supervision of Mantegna himself. Documents record the proces-
sion which escorted the *Altarpiece*
from the artist's workshop to the
church and the admiration it caused.
The enthroned Virgin with the
Child standing on her lap are strongly
reminiscent of the *Madonna* in the
Brera; and E. Tietze-Conrat infers
that Mary's gesture may be derived
from Leonardo's *Madonna of the
Rocks*. On either side of the Virgin
are SS Michael, Andrew, Longinus,
and George, and an old woman
variously identified as St Elizabeth,
St Anne, or Osanna, a pious woman
of that time; kneeling on the left is
Francesco Gonzaga (plate 133); on
the pedestal are Adam and Eve and
the serpent. The altarpiece was taken
away by the French in 1797. Lanzi
praises its smooth design, but Crowe
and Cavalcaselle think that the dis-
proportion of the figures and a
certain hardness of treatment in
places are due to the work of an
assistant, perhaps Francesco Mantegna.

A drawing of the same dimensions
and mechanically similar to this canvas is in the Ducal Palace in Mantua.
Ozzola published it (*Civiltà*, 1942)
as a working design for this painting
executed by Mantegna himself.
Fiocco (*Rivista d'Arte*, 1942) said
that it was traced from the original
in the Neo-classic Age before the
removal of the altarpiece to France,
and furthermore the Castle's inven-
tories do not mention the cartoon.
E. Tietze-Conrat, on the other hand,
considers the drawing a development of the artist's original idea and
so "interesting as unique evidence of
a stage in the working process."

Fiocco's theory seems the most convincing.

Plate 133
MADONNA DELLA VITTORIA. Detail: Francesco Gonzaga.

Plate 134
VIRGIN AND CHILD WITH ST JOHN THE BAPTIST AND MARY MAGDALEN. *Canvas, 138 × 116.5. London, National Gallery.* Signed: ANDREAS MANTINIA C.P.F. The last three letters are generally interpreted as *Civis Patavinus Fecit*, although Davies reads them as *Comes Patavinus Fecit*, recalling that Mantegna had been created a Count by Pope Innocent VIII for the work he had done in the Vatican and that he had signed himself as such in the Papel Chapel. Apparently this canvas once hung in the chapel of the Monti Palace in Milan. We know it was owned by Cardinal Cesare Monti, an Archbishop of Milan (1632–50), and was brought to London after the purchase of the Roverselli Collection. A. Venturi considers it to have been painted before the *Madonna della Vittoria*, and E. Tietze-Conrat suggests in or about 1500. Together with Crowe and Cavalcaselle and Fiocco, E. Tietze-Conrat assumes the workshop collaborated in the execution because of the rather mediocre inventiveness and dry brushwork. However, the aridity and harshness of the pinks are typical of Mantegna's late works.

Plate 135
MADONNA AND CHILD WITH FOUR SAINTS. *Canvas, 287 × 214. Milan, Civico Museo del Castello Sforzesco.* The book held by the angel is inscribed: A. MANTINIA PI. AN. GRACIE 1497, 15 AUGUSTJ. Formerly above the high altar of the Church of Santa Maria in Organo at Verona, then in the Trivulzio Collection in Milan, from where it passed to its present location. Though identification is not absolutely certain, the saints around the throne are thought to be John the Baptist, Gregory, Benedict, and Jerome. The work was recently cleaned and restored by Pellicioli. (See also plates 136 and 137.)

Plate 136
MADONNA AND CHILD WITH FOUR SAINTS. Detail: the angels below.

Plate 137
MADONNA AND CHILD WITH FOUR SAINTS. Detail: busts of SS Benedict and Jerome.

Plate 138
MADONNA AND CHILD. *Canvas, 43 × 31. Bergamo, Accademia Carrara.* Presented to the Academy by Count Marenzi in 1831. Early critics assigned it to the Padua period, but Crowe and Cavalcaselle thought it was painted after the *Triumphs of Caesar*. Arslan considers it close in time to the *St Euphemia* in Naples. E. Tietze-Conrat believes it was probably executed shortly before Mantegna's move to Mantua. Gilbert considers it datable around the time of *Carlo de' Medici* (1466). Longhi attributes it correctly to the artist's last years.

Plate 139
MADONNA AND CHILD WITH THE INFANT ST JOHN AND SAINTS. *Canvas, 75.5 × 61.5. Dresden, Gemäldegalerie.* From the Sir Charles Eastlake Collection in London. In the seventeenth century, it may possibly have belonged to Bernardo Giunto of Venice, and it is mentioned by Ridolfi in 1648. Crowe and Cavalcaselle think this may be

the painting executed for Eleanor of Aragon. The two saints on either side of Mary are Joachim and Anne. The figure of the Infant St John is vaguely suggestive of Leonardo's manner.

Plate 140

THE HOLY FAMILY WITH ST JOHN (The Infant Christ as Ruler of the World). *Canvas, 75 × 50.5. London, National Gallery.* From the Manga Collection at Verona the work passed to the Mond Collection in London and from there to its present location. The Christ Child is represented as Ruler of the World, holding the Orbs. He and St John are standing on a well in the garden described in the Song of Songs (see Roger Fry in *The Burlington Magazine*, 1905). Next to them are the Virgin, who appears to be sewing, and St Joseph, his head turned aside. The work was painted over in several places and first restored by Cavenaghi who put a book in the Virgin's hand. This addition was removed in the course of restoration (1946–8) when the painting entered the Gallery.

Color Plate VIII

THE DEAD CHRIST. Detail of plate 130: the body of Christ.

Plate 141

CHRIST SEATED ON A SARCOPHAGUS AND SUPPORTED BY TWO ANGELS. *Panel, 83 × 51. Copenhagen, Statens Museum for Kunst.* Signed on the throne's pedestal, at the right: ANDREAS MANTINIA. Formerly in the collection of Cardinal Valenti, Secretary to Pope Benedict XIV (eighteenth century). Another

version of this composition is mentioned in an inventory of Mantua Castle compiled in 1627. Fiocco thinks that the panel might have been executed in Rome. E. Tietze-Conrat dates the painting in the middle or second half of the 1490's.

Plate 142

ST SEBASTIAN. *Canvas, 210 × 91. Venice, Ca' d'Oro.* Inscribed on the scroll attached to the candle on the lower right: NIHIL NISI DIVINVM STABILE EST, COETERA FUMUS. As recalled by Lodovico Mantegna in his letter of October 2, 1506, this work was in Mantegna's study at the time of his death. It was presumably painted for Lodovico Gonzaga, Bishop of Mantua; later it belonged to Cardinal Bembo in Padua, then to the Gradenigo family; Baron Franchetti bought it from the Scarpa Collection in Motta di Livenza and presented it to the Ca' d'Oro. Pallucchini (*I capolavori dei musei veneti*, 1946) states that it was executed toward the end of the fifteenth century for Sigismondo Gonzaga who, however, did not become Bishop of Mantua until 1511. E. Tietze-Conrat and Arslan are inclined to consider it close in time to the *Triumphs of Caesar*, but I believe it was painted later. Fiocco has written that this work "represents the highest point of what we may describe as the master's linear metaphysics, which go beyond the functional design of the Tuscans."

Plate 143

THE HOLY FAMILY WITH A FEMALE SAINT. *Canvas, 72 × 55. Verona, Museo di Castelvecchio.* This painting is said to have been given by the Bernasconi family of Verona to the Church of the Incurabili in Venice, where it was seen by Boschini in 1674. It was later returned to Verona and acquired for the museum. Kristeller, Thode, Knapp, Frizzoni, and A. Venturi ascribed it to a follower of Mantegna, but Morelli, supported later by Berenson, Fiocco and Pallucchino, attributed it to Mantegna. E. Tietze-Conrat thinks it could have been painted by Francesco Bonsignori. There are similar treatments of this subject: a canvas in Dresden (plate 139), a picture in the Metropolitan Museum in New York, one in the Musée Jacquemart-André in Paris and a *Madonna with St Julian* in Castelvecchio itself. Restoration carried out in 1946 has revealed beyond all doubt the extent of Mantegna's powers toward the end of his career.

Plate 144

THE TRIUMPH OF SCIPIO. *Canvas, 73 × 268. London, National Gallery.* This is a monochrome in poor condition and has been cut in two. The left half is reproduced in this plate. Rather than the *Triumph of Scipio* it represents the introduction in Rome of the cult-image of the Phrygian Mother of the Gods, Cybele, from whom the Cornelii claimed descent. The Cornaros, in their turn, considered themselves the descendants of the Cornelii. Mantegna was given the commission for this work by Francesco Cornaro in 1504. However, due to a disagreement over the price, the painting was not delivered. It was probably part of a larger decorative scheme including the two panels of *Tucia* and *Sophonisba*, also in the National Gallery, and the *Continence of Scipio*, painted by Giovanni Bellini after Mantegna's death and now in the Kress Collec-

tion. This was proved by Longhi in *Vita Artistica* (1927) but E. Tietze-Conrat does not accept this reconstruction. The painting was kept for some time by Francesco Mantegna who wished to study it, and then went to Cardinal Scipione and later passed into the Cornaro Collection. It was hung in the Cornaro palace in Campo San Paolo until 1815, when it became the property of the Sanquirico family who sold it in 1873 to Captain Ralph Vivian. Fiocco thinks it might have been painted immediately after the artist's return from Rome.

Plate 145

THE TRIUMPH OF SCIPIO. The right half.

Plate 146a

THE VESTAL VIRGIN TUCCIA WITH A SIEVE. *Panel, 72.5 × 23. London, National Gallery.* Executed against a marbled background and inscribed on the back ANDREA MANTEGNA. The subject was formerly thought to be an allegory of Autumn, rather than the Vestal Tuccia who, according to legend, carried some water from the Tiber in a sieve as proof of her innocence. This could be the picture catalogued as No. 17 in the Bertles Sale in April, 1775. It reached its present location in 1882 with *Sophonisba* (plate 146b), after the sale of the Hamilton Collection. Both works were believed to be fakes by Morelli and Frizzoni. E. Tietze-Conrat thinks they were probably executed by an artist in Mantegna's workshop, though she lists them as essays in the master's style, is inclined to attribute them to Mantegna. A. Venturi points out the fine execution of both paintings. (See comment on plate 144.)

Plate 146b

SOPHONISBA. *Panel, 72.5 × 23. London, National Gallery.* The mythical African Queen is represented drinking poison to avoid the humiliation of being taken back to Rome as a prisoner. The subject has also been interpreted as an allegory of Summer. (See comment on previous plate.)

Plate 147

SAMSON AND DELILAH. *Canvas, 47 × 37. London, National Gallery.* Monochrome imitation of a bas-relief on pink marble ground. The tree trunk is inscribed: FOEMINA DIABOLO TRIBVS ASSIBVS EST MALA PEIOR. The work reached its present location after the sale of the Sunderland drawings. This is the finest of a series of monochromes of equal dimensions consisting of the Dublin *Judith* (plate 160), the *David* (plate 174), the *Sacrifice of Abraham* (plate 175) both in Vienna and the *Judgment of Solomon* in the Louvre.

Plate 148

JUDITH. *Canvas, 64 × 30. Montreal, Art Association.* This painting and its companion *Dido* were part of the John E. Taylor Collection in London. Both works are monochromes, brownish with golden-yellow lights, on a gray marble ground. Kristeller thought them both to be workshop productions. E. Tietze-Conrat, supported by Paccagnini, refuses to ascribe them to Mantegna, but all other critics accept the attribution. Indeed the relationship E. Tietze-Conrat noted between this *Judith* and the fresco in Mantegna's chapel in the Church of Sant'Andrea in Mantua is sufficient proof that the monochrome has a higher standard of inventiveness and execution.

Plate 149

DIDO. *Canvas, 64 × 30. Montreal, Art Association.* (See comment on plate 148.)

Plate 150

PARNASSUS. *Canvas, 160 × 192. Paris, Louvre.* Painted for Isabella d'Este's study in the Ducal Palace in Mantua. The frame, carved under Mantegna's supervision, together with that of the *Triumph of Virtue*, are still kept in the palace. On July 5, 1497, Alberto da Bologna wrote to Isabella saying that the painting had already been hung in her study. It must have been the first of several mythological subjects Isabella commissioned from different artists. These pictures were subsequently all bought by Cardinal Richelieu for his castle at Du Plessis, and *Parnassus* entered the Louvre in 1881. The subject is clearly indicated in an inventory of the Ducal Palace compiled in 1542: "Mars and a Venus in a moment of pleasure, with Vulcan, an Orpheus playing, and nine dancing Nymphs." The traditional title of *Parnassus* is therefore inaccurate. In 1948 E. Wind published a complicated but unconvincing interpretation both of the painting and of Isabella's plans for decorating her study. E. Tietze-Conrat rejected the interpretation in *Art Bulletin* (1949). Fiocco remarks that "here all torment is stilled, due to a rhythm that was to remain unrivaled until the advent of Raphael." Recent cleaning has emphasized the fine execution, especially the landscape—although this is not typical of Mantegna's style, as only Gilbert seems to have noticed.

Plate 151

THE TRIUMPH OF VIRTUE. *Canvas, 160 × 192. Paris, Louvre.* Possibly the second allegorical subject for

Isabella d'Este's study, and executed in or about 1502. The picture has the same provenance as the *Parnassus*. Forster thinks the subject represents Minerva expelling the Vices—seen as satyrs—from the paths of Virtue. This is also indicated in the words inscribed on the scroll around the olive tree at the left.

Isabella d'Este dated July 15, 1506, states that Mantegna painted the god with two figures of women. The picture was finished by Costa and he must have reorganized the whole composition to suit his own ideas. The theme illustrated here has been analyzed by Wind and E. Tietze-Conrat.

Plate 152

COMUS, THE GOD OF REVELRY. *Canvas, 160 × 238. Paris, Louvre.* Begun by Mantegna shortly before his death. A letter from Calandra to

Plate 153

COMUS, THE GOD OF REVELRY. Detail: the group of goddesses on the right.

LOST PAINTINGS

The following includes only lost works that are mentioned in sources and documents from the fifteenth to the seventeenth centuries:

BASSANO

A painting, the subject of which is unknown, possibly on a wall of the Church of San Bernardino. Mentioned by Lanzi (*Storia pittorica dell'Italia*, Bassano, 1795–96).

BERLIN

The Flagellation, in the Royal Castle. Painted for Barbara of Brandenburg and presented by the Count of Ayala to the Queen of Prussia (*Memoires de l'Académie Royale des Sciences et Belles Lettres*, Berlin 1805).

BOLOGNA

The Dead Christ, in Casa Zacconi, previously De Lodi. Mentioned by Lamo (*La graticola di Bologna* [1560], Bologna, 1844). "Mantegna's *Presepio*," in the Galleria Bonfiglioli. Mentioned in a 1757 inventory (Campori).

FERRARA

A small panel with the *Portrait of Lionello d'Este* on one side and the *Portrait of Folco di Villafora* on the reverse. (See Biographical Notes, 1449, May 23.)

"A painting on wood of the sorrowful Marys by the hand of Andrea Mantegna." From a 1493 inventory of the d'Este Castle.

"A painting on wood of Our Lady and the Child with Seraphim, by the hand of the above-mentioned Mantegna." From the inventory and possibly to be identified with the *Virgin and Child with Cherubim* in Milan. (See comment on plate 128.)

A *Nativity of Christ*, in the Chapel of Duchess Margherita Gonzaga. Recorded by Campori "Pittori Estensi," in *Atti . . . della Deputazione di storia patria*, III. Regarding the identification of this work with the *Adoration of the Shepherds* in New York, see comment on plate 44.

Christ Among the Doctors. In the above-mentioned chapel, and recorded by Campori.

A *Death of Our Lady*. In the above-mentioned chapel, and recorded by Campori. Regarding the identification of this work with the *Death of the Virgin* in Madrid see comment on plate 76.

A picture of uncertain subject in the above-mentioned chapel, and recorded by Campori.

A *Dead Christ . . .* "placed upon a chair next to a building in ruins and in a landscape with animals and birds; and He is being watched by two old people who are seated and almost naked." In the collection of Count Roberto Canonici and destroyed by fire in 1638. Recorded in a 1632 inventory published by Campori who, however, pointed out that some of the works collected by Canonici were of doubtful origin.

A *Dead Christ . . .* "lying on a bier in the middle of a landscape; next to him is an old man sitting by a tree; St John is represented weeping and the Virgin has fainted in the arms of a woman; there are also mountains, rocks, cemeteries and grottoes, above which are two shepherds, one sitting and the other playing the pipe; two old men are opening a grave and another is carrying a basin. There are also some skulls of men, dogs, cats and birds, and several figures of resurrected people." In the Canonici Collection, and recorded in the 1632 inventory.

A painting "by the hand of Mantegna, with sixteen children dancing and playing instruments. It is inscribed above: 'Melancholy.' It has a gilded frame 14 *on.** high and 20 and a half *on.* wide." The work belonged to Cesare Ignazio d'Este. Mentioned in a 1685 inventory of the Prince's property (Campori).

FIESOLE
". . . a half-length figure of Our Lady with the Child in her arms, and heads of angels singing, which are painted with infinite grace, for the Abbot of the Abbey of Fiesole." The description is by Vasari, and he recorded that the picture was then "in the library of the abbey and has always been considered a rare work of beauty." This painting has occasionally been identified with the *Virgin and Child with Cherubim* in the Brera (see comment on plate 128), but the latter probably came from Ferrara. Crowe and Cavalcaselle tentatively identified it with a *Madonna* in Berlin, now attributed to Lazzaro Bastiani.

FLORENCE
Half-lengths of the Virgin and Child with St John and Two Saints, the property of "Signor Bernardo Giunti, a gentleman from Florence." Mentioned by Ridolfi.

LONDON
A *Madonna and Child with Six Saints*, in the collection of King Charles I. From the catalogue of a sale at Somerset House (May, 1650).

MANTUA
Panels for the Palace Chapel. See Biographical Notes 1464, April 26. Vasari may be describing these when he refers to "a small panel . . . the figures in this work are not very large but are exceedingly beautiful." Regarding the identification of these panels with the *Florence Triptych* see comment on plates 72–73.

"Historia del Limbo" (The Legend of Limbo). See Biographical Notes (1468, July 27). A small version of this subject is mentioned in an inventory of the contents of Mantua Castle compiled in or about 1700. (See comment on plate 154.)

Portraits of Emperor Frederick III and Christian, King of Denmark. Mentioned by Mario Equicola (*Chronica di Mantova*, 1521) who thought, however, that the portraits were more likely to have represented two of the figures in the *Camera degli Sposi*.

Portraits of the Marquis Lodovico of Mantua and his Wife, Barbara of Brandenburg. See Biographical Notes (1477, July 6). Perhaps once part of the collection of the artist, Nicola Renier, in Venice, which was dispersed in 1666 (A. Segarizzi, *Nuovo Archivio Veneto*, 1914). Two similar portraits were later in the Hamilton Collection in Glasgow and considered to be copies by Crowe and Cavalcaselle and Kristeller. They

* The measurement *onciale* (abbreviated *on.*) was equal to roughly 20 centimeters.

were auctioned in Paris in 1900 with the Collection Cernuschi and are now lost.

Portrait of Isabella d'Este. See Biographical Notes (1493, January 12).

The Triumphs of Petrarch. See Biographical Notes (1501, February 13).

". . . a picture of four figures in bronze color, by the hand of Andrea Mantegna." Mentioned in a 1542 inventory of the art collection of Isabella d'Este (D'Arco).

". . . another picture in bronze color also by Mantegna with a ship at sea, some figures inside it, and one falling into the water." From the 1542 inventory.

Christ and the Samaritan Woman. In a letter dated November 1549 to Cardinal Ercole Gonzaga, Timoteo de' Giusti asked for a copy of this work (Mantua, Archivio Gonzaga).

Our Lord Being Placed in the Sepulcher, a foreshortened composition within a gilded frame, in the Ducal Palace. From a 1612 inventory (D'Arco).

". . . Four gouache paintings by the hand of Andrea Mantegna: one portrays Tobias, another Esther, a third Abraham, and the fourth Moses. They have black frames decorated with gold." In the Ducal Palace, and recorded in the same inventory.

"A canvas with our Lord and the Woman taken in Adultery, in half-lengths, without a frame, by the hand of Andrea Mantegna." In the Ducal Palace, and recorded in the same source.

". . . a dance portrayed by Andrea Mantegna in the Grotto." In the Ducal Palace, and recorded in the same inventory.

". . . a panel . . . stolen by the Germans during the sack of that city in 1630," painted for Marquis Lodovico Gonzaga. Mentioned by Ridolfi.

". . . upon the pulpit (Andrea Mantegna) painted St Louis, King of France," in the Church of San Francesco. Mentioned by Ridolfi.

"*Our Lord on His Way to Egypt*: an original by Andrea Mantegna," belonging to Charles II of Mantua. Mentioned in a 1665 inventory of the art collection of Charles II, Duke of Mantua (D'Arco).

"a portrait painted by Mantegna." In the Ducal Palace. From an inventory of about 1700 (D'Arco). The picture is listed as measuring about "one arm" in length.

". . . a smaller [than the previous] painting, by Mantegna, showing Christ in Limbo." In the Ducal Palace, and recorded in the same source.

"*A Man with a Boy Carrying his Arrows,*" an obvious sign of Mantegna's activities about ten years after the *Camera degli Sposi.*" Painted on the ceiling of the Scalcheria. Mentioned by Crowe and Cavalcaselle. "Upon the exterior [of the facade of Sant'Andrea] he painted the Apostles watching Savior ascending to Heaven." Mentioned by Ridolfi. (See Biographical Notes (1488).)

Mantegna's own decoration of this house "which adjoins San Sebastiano and has his name carved upon it on a stone, but the paintings were destroyed by the Germans." Mentioned by Ridolfi.

NAPLES
The Entombment, in the Church of San Domenico. Mentioned in a letter by Summonte to Michiel dated 1524.

NOVELLARA
"*A Child Clothed,* 20 *on.* high, 10 *on.* wide, by Mantegna." In the Casa

Gonzaga. Mentioned in an inventory compiled in 17 . . . (Campori).

"A *Triumph* in watercolor, 14 *on.* high, 8 *on.* wide, by Mantegna." In the Casa Gonzaga and recorded by Campori.

"*A Monarch Enthroned, Surrounded by his Courtiers*, a watercolor drawing." Recorded by Campori.

PADUA

Altarpiece for the Church of Santa Sofia. See Biographical Notes (1448, October 16). Mentioned by Vasari, Scardeone, and others. Destroyed before 1648 (Boschini).

Portraits of Janus Pannonius and Galeotto Marzio of Narni. Presumably painted in Padua. Mentioned by Pannonius in his *Laus Andreae Mantegnae pictoris Patavini*, written before 1458.

Portrait of Girolamo Valle, in the Church of the Eremitani. Mentioned by Scardeone. Possibly one of the figures in the *Martyrdom of St Christopher*.

St Benedict, "a canvas in the choir of the Church of San Benedetto." Mentioned by Michiel.

The Savior sending forth the Apostles in the Church of the Spirito Santo. Mentioned by Ridolfi.

"Particular paintings which at various times were transported elsewhere." Mentioned by Ridolfi.

The History of Gattamelata, painted on the front of a house near Santa Lucia. Mentioned by Scardeone. About 1524 Paola Giovio, who wrote a biography of Gattamelata, had stated that Mantegna had painted a *Mourning over the Dead Condottiero*. The reader is referred to E. Tietze-Conrat (*Mantegna*, London, 1955) for a possible reconstruction of this

painting through an engraving in the Wallace Collection, London—although its relationship to Mantegna is difficult to see.

In addition to the lost works listed above, the following were destroyed as a result of air-raids on March 11, 1944 and are illustrated in plates 1–7, 22–23 (see relevant comments): *Head of a Colossus, St Peter, St Paul, St Christopher*, the *Calling of SS James and John, St James Expelling the Demons*, the *Baptism of Hermogenes, St James Before Herod Agrippa, St James Healing the Crippled Man* and the *Martyrdom of St James* (this last work has been partly restored). All these frescoes were formerly in the Ovetari Chapel in the Church of the Eremitani in Padua.

PARMA

"*A Man ascending Steps with a Candle, and Other Figures* in the Palazzo del Giardino. The picture is 1 *br.,** 4 *on.* high and 11 *on.* wide." From an inventory of about 1680 (Campori).

"A canvas on wood, 1 *br.*, 6 *on.* high, and 1 *br.*, 30 *on.* wide, with the sketch of a woman, perhaps Susannah, and two old men. It is entirely perished and said to be by Mantegna." In the Palazzo del Giardino, and mentioned by Campori.

REGGIO EMILIA

"*The Judgment of Solomon*, a gouache by Andrea Mantegna." In the study of Bishop Coccapani. From an inventory of about 1640 (Campori). This could be a monochrome now in the Louvre (see Paintings Attributed to Mantegna).

"A head of a Man in the manner of

* 1 Braccia: roughly the length of an arm.

Mantegna." Also in the Coccapani study. Mentioned in the 1640 inventory (Campori).

ROME

"Seven panels with the life, miracles and martyrdom of St Sebastian. They are well painted and in good condition, the figures being just under two *palmi** in height. The figures, the architecture and the landscapes are all by Mantegna. The panels are all of the same size, that is to say 3 and ¼ *palmi* in height and 2 and ¼ *palmi* in width. The frames are also all alike and they are smooth, in the Roman style." These panels belonged to Queen Christina of Sweden, and are mentioned in a catalogue of her pictures compiled in or about 1689. They later became part of the Odescalchi Collection.

VATICAN CITY

Frescoes in the Chapel of Innocent VIII in the Belvedere, the Vatican. These were painted in a small chapel, about 8 × 8 feet and in a smaller adjoining sacristy in the garden house built by Innocent VIII at the far end of the Belvedere courtyard. The sacristy was decorated with a "false ledge supporting small cupboards in which one can see chalices, ciboriums, crosses, candelabra, and other sacred vessels. All round the cupboards, the pilasters and frieze (simulated by Mantegna on the walls and ceiling of the sacristy) there runs a Chinese ornament on a gold (or blue) ground."† The entrance to the actual chapel was decorated with the arms of Innocent VIII. As one entered to the right of the door, one saw an altar of white marble above which was a "fresco of *St John Baptizing the Redeemer*, who is escorted by angels carrying his robes. On the two sides are other figures and one of them is seated in the act of removing his stocking. A cheerful landscape and a city are visible in the background. Above this painting there is a representation of *The Holy Ghost* beneath two festoons of fruit with a golden scroll in the center. On the opposite wall, at the left of the door, there is a window . . . in the ogive of which and against a blue ground some cherubs are seen holding a golden oval inscribed: INNOCENT VIII. P.M, DEDICATED [THIS CHAPEL] TO HIS PREDECESSOR, ST JOHN THE BAPTIST, IN THE YEAR 1490. On the remaining part of the wall, below the frieze, one may admire the *Annunciation and the Holy Ghost*, both painted against a similar background. Upon the wall facing the door there are many soldiers taking part in the *Beheading of St John the Baptist* who is seen waiting patiently for the executioner's sword to fall upon him. Above this scene a painted frieze represents the *Dance of Herodias' Daughter*, with several figures busily preparing the feast in a garden and a magnificent cupboard in the center, inside which there are some gold plates. Opposite this wall, that is to say on either side of the entrance door, are painted half-length figures of *St Anthony Abbot, St Paul the Hermit, St Stephen, and St Lawrence*; above them is the *Adoration of the Magi* and highest of all the *Nativity*. Over the door there is a great fresco of the *Madonna and Child*

---

* 1 *Palmo*: roughly the distance between the tips of the thumb and little finger measured with the hand fully open.

† All the quotations on these frescoes are from G. P. Chattard: *Nuova Descrizione del Vaticano.*

with SS Paul, John, and Katherine at the right and on the left *SS Peter, Andrew* and the above-mentioned Pontiff, who is kneeling, and behind him are other *Virgin Saints*, the whole group being beautifully expressed."

The four lunettes contained two Virtues each and in the fourth there was a chiaroscuro of the *Sacrifice of Abraham*. The Virtues were *Faith, Hope, Charity*, and *Discretion*, the latter represented by an old woman, above the window; on the opposite wall, that is above the altar, were *Prudence, Justice, Temperance*, and *Fortitude*. "Nor should one be surprised that, through the caprice of his invention, the artist who painted such beautiful things should have placed *Discretion* among the most heroic of Virtues. The Abbot Taja, in his *Description of the Vatican Palace* (page 406), relates that the wise professor (Mantegna), finding that his needs were increasing every day and that the Pope, occupied with his numerous avocations, had forgotten him, decided to express his condition of want in such a silent form of language. Whereupon the Pontiff, going one day to see the work, inquired of Andrea what that figure might be. To which the artist replied: "Holy Father, that is Discretion." The Pope rejoined: "If thou wouldst have her to be well accompanied, set Patience beside her."* In the spandrels the *Four Evangelists* are painted in airy space and the spandrels sustain the golden frame of the highest cupola. This is decorated with a number of *tondi*, interconnected in the manner of a reticule, and the latter is interrupted by fifteen cherubs holding garlands of fruit; at the summit of this ensemble one can see the arms of Pope Innocent VIII. Here and there, heads of cherubs ennoble this masterly work devised and executed by that celebrated artist from Mantua, Andrea Mantegna, who painted the whole chapel with no other help but himself, as seen by the inscription that he left on the right and left sides of the large window that I have described. The floor is covered with a mosaic of many colors, divided into five *tondi* inside a great square. Stars can be seen in the four lateral *tondi* and in the center one are the arms of the above-mentioned Pontiff Innocent VIII." (G. P. Chattard, *Nuova Descrizione del Vaticano*, Rome, 1762–7; also extensively described by Vasari, and by A. Taya, *Descrizione del Palazzo Apostolico*, Rome, 1750.)

VENICE

". . . a small painting representing *Mucius Scaevola Burning his Own Hand.*" In the house of Francesco Zio. Mentioned by Michiel in a *Notizia* of 1512.

". . . a small painting of the story of St Christopher, done by Mantegna in Padua, in the Church of the Eremitani, a most beautiful work." In the house of Michele Contarini. Mentioned by Michiel in a *Notizia* of August 1543.

"A half-length painting of Our Lord carrying the Cross." Mentioned by Michiel (Cicogna, "Intorno alla vita di M. A. Michiel," in *Memorie dell' Istituto Veneto*, 1860).

"A painting with the head of St Jerome. The frame is white." Mentioned by Michiel, as above.

A number of works in the study of Ottavio de' Tassis. Mentioned by F. Sansovino (*Venezia Descritta*, Venice, 1581).

* This anecdote is related by Vasari (*Lives of the Artists*, 1568).

VERONA

Altarpiece of SS Christopher and Anthony. Mentioned by Vasari.

"*The Seven Deadly Sins,* painted with golden lights." In the study of Muselli. From a 1662 inventory (Campori).

Portrait of Mattio Bossi. Mentioned by Maffei (*Verona Illustrata,* Verona, 1731).

Frescoes on a house in the Piazza del Lago. Mentioned by Ridolfi.

UNCERTAIN LOCATION

"*A Portrait of Marquis Lodovico of Mantua,* on wood." Mentioned by Campori.

PAINTINGS ATTRIBUTED TO MANTEGNA

Plate 154

CHRIST DESCENDING INTO HELL. *Panel, 71 × 55.5. Formerly in Asolo, Valier Collection.* This painting is at present on the market. On July 27, 1468, Mantegna informed Marquis Lodovico that he had begun a painting of Limbo. This, however, for stylistic reasons, could not have been the picture reproduced here, which was published by Fiocco as an original work belonging to Mantegna's late period, completed in the upper part by Correggio. Another version of the lower part is in the Stephen Courtauld Collection at Taynuilt (Argyll) and yet another one, though mediocre and executed later, is in the Pinacoteca in Bologna. That the original idea was Mantegna's seems to be confirmed by an eighteenth-century engraving bearing the initials A.M., and the date 1492, but the execution does not appear to be by Mantegna.

Plate 155

SACRA CONVERSAZIONE. *Panel, 56 × 43. Boston, Massachusetts, Isabella Stewart Gardner Museum.* Fiocco believes the signature, ANDREVS MANTINIA, is a later addition. From the collection of Charles I, the picture passed to the Royal Spanish Court and later to Prince Drago from whom Isabella Stewart Gardner acquired it. It was originally in Ferrara at the Court of Margherita Gonzaga (see comments on plates 76 and 44) and that is possibly

where Bastiano Filippi reduced it to its present dimensions which match those of the Prado's *Death of the Virgin* (plate 76). Longhi (1934 and 1962) is probably right in considering it an autograph work, and he assigns it to Mantegna's last years. Fiocco found it difficult to judge the painting because of its damaged condition. E. Tietze-Conrat ascribes it to a Ferrarese artist and dates it about 1480, which is too early.

Plate 156

MADONNA AND CHILD. *Canvas, 43 × 34. Basel, Private Collection.* Signed: OPVS ANDREAE MANTEGNAE. Published by Fiocco (*The Burlington Magazine*, 1949) as an early work of 1452, when the artist was still strongly influenced by Piero della Francesca. E. Tietze-Conrat considers it made up of parts copied from other pictures by Mantegna.

Plate 157

VIRGIN AND CHILD WITH CHERUBIM. *Panel, 79 × 67. Berlin, Staatliches Museen.* Accepted as an original by Kristeller and by Crowe and Cavalcaselle, and linked with the *Madonna and Child with Cherubim* in New York (plate 31). Berenson considered it a copy of an early Mantegna. Earlier, Sandberg-Vavala had correctly ascribed it to Lazzaro Bastiani (*The Burlington Magazine*) and was supported by Collobi (*Critica d'arte*, 1949) and Longhi (1962). Coletti includes this panel among the works variously attributed to Bastiani, Quirizio da Murano and to a follower of either Bartolomeo Vivarini or Fra' Antonio da Negroponte, or even to a pupil of Murano. The work, however, was still being exhibited as an early Mantegna in 1951.

Plate 158a

MADONNA AND CHILD. *Panel, 87 × 76. Invergarry (Scotland), William U. Goodbody Collection.* Formerly in Bologna, the property of Podio, an antique-dealer. Acquired by Agnew and published—while still on the market—by Roger Fry as a work by Mantegna derived from bas-reliefs by Donatello. The attribution was confirmed by Fiocco and Coletti and rejected by E. Tietze-Conrat. The panel has been repainted and is now being presented as an unfinished work. It is difficult to imagine it as belonging to Mantegna's œuvre at any stage of his development.

Plate 158b

MADONNA AND CHILD. *Panel, 48 × 34.5. Boston, Museum of Fine Arts.* From an unidentified castle in Brandenburg it passed to its present location in 1933. The attribution to Mantegna is accepted by Fiocco, and he dates it at the same time as the Ovetari Chapel frescoes. Berenson omits it from his list; Suida believes this work and the *Holy Family and a Female Saint* in Verona to be by a pupil; E. Tietze-Conrat ascribes it to a follower of the early Mantegna. I am inclined to suggest an imitator, such as Bastiani, who elaborated the motifs of Donatello, which were young Mantegna's favorites.

Plate 159

THE HOLY FAMILY WITH ST JOHN THE BAPTIST AND HIS PARENTS. *Canvas, 40 × 169. Mantua, Church of Sant'Andrea, Mantegna's Chapel (first on the left).* This painting and the *Baptism of Christ,* in the same church, have been identified by some with "the two pictures destined for the Chapel" mentioned by Lodovico Mantegna in his letter dated October 2, 1506, to Marquis Gonzaga, in which he listed the works left by his late father. This canvas obviously represents a composition derived from Mantegna. It may possibly have been executed by the artist's son, Francesco (who died not long after his father), or by the same follower who painted the *Holy Family with a Female Saint* in the Metropolitan Museum, New York. The *Baptism of Christ,* considered by Fiocco a workshop-replica of the fresco in the Chapel of Innocent VIII, is mediocre, and differs from documented descriptions of the Vatican frescoes. In my opinion E. Tietze-Conrat is correct in saying that not even its conception is typical of Mantegna. Paccagnini attributes the *Baptism of Christ* to Francesco Mantegna, and believes he painted it about 1515, because of its analogies with *Christ Carrying the Cross* in Verona (plate 173). But one cannot be certain, however, that Francesco painted this last work. The decoration of the Chapel in Sant' Andrea was begun immediately after Mantegna's death and was completed in 1516. The four figures of the Evangelists in the Spandrels were traditionally ascribed to Correggio's early period, and A. Venturi accepted this attribution.

Plate 160

JUDITH. *Canvas, 46 × 35. Dublin, National Gallery of Ireland.* The composition of this monochrome is similar to an engraving by Zoan Andrea and to that of the Montreal painting (plate 148) which—according to E. Tietze-Conrat—is derived from this *Judith.* But the quality of this work is surely inferior. Berenson, Fiocco and Paccagnini accept it as an autograph painting but qualify their attribution by saying that Mantegna must have executed it when he was very tired. A. Venturi considers it definitely a workshop production.

Plate 161

OCCASIO AND PAENITENTIA. *Fresco transferred to canvas, 168 × 146. Mantua, Museo del Palazzo Ducale.* From a fireplace in the house of Marchese Biondi in Mantua. The subject-matter has been variously interpreted. All evidence seems to point to a pupil of Mantegna, possibly, as Kristeller suggested, Antonio da Pavia.

Plate 162

ST MARK. *Canvas, 82 × 63.5. Frankfurt-am-Main, Staedelsches Kunstinstitut.* Acquired in Paris in 1867. Inscribed: INCLITA MAGNANIMI VE . . . EVANGELISTA. PAX TIBI . . . ANDREAE MANTEGNAE . . . O . . . LABOR. The authenticity of the inscription is not unanimously accepted. Fiocco thought it was genuine but he at first attributed the execution to Pizzolo; Berenson ascribed it definitely to Mantegna; E. Tietze-Conrat thinks it was painted by an artist of the Paduan School, who apart from the same background, had nothing in common with Mantegna. Though several artists have been suggested for this canvas, Fiocco's theory seems the most likely, on the grounds that the execution recalls Pizzolo's work in the Ovetari Chapel. On the other hand, if the inscription were indeed found to be genuine, one would have to agree with Longhi who places it (1962) among Mantegna's earliest works.

Plate 163

PORTRAIT OF A GENTLEMAN. *Panel, 33 × 25. Milan, Poldi Pezzoli*

Museum. The origins are uncertain. Attributed to Cosmé Tura by Bertini in 1881. In 1894 Berenson, who noted some Mantegna elements, ascribed the panel to Francesco Bonsignori. This opinion was generally accepted and is still shared by Paccagnini. Morassi (1936) is inclined to attribute it to a Ferrarese artist. Suida (1946) and Longhi (1962) are definitely in favor of Mantegna, and Russoli (1955)—together with most contemporary critics—considers it very close in manner to Mantegna. Coletti (1953), however, assigns it to Gentile Bellini under the influence of Pisanello.

Plate 164

ST BERNARDINO. *Canvas, 385 × 220. Milan, Brera Gallery.* A scroll in the lower part of the picture bears a date that appears to have been repainted. It reads 1460, but Fiocco—attributing this practically ruined canvas to Mantegna—reads it 1468. Although acknowledged as partly original also by Longhi (1962), this work is generally ascribed to Mantegna's workshop.

Plate 165

THE DEATH OF THE VIRGIN. *Mosaic, Venice, Basilica di San Marco, Mascoli Chapel.* A most controversial work so far as an attribution to Mantegna is concerned, but also extremely interesting as a possible link between Tuscan and Venetian painting. Thode (1898) thought the composition so much more modern than those of the other two mosaics in the same chapel that he believed Andrea del Castagno may have intervened in the work. At the same time he was struck by the resemblance between this *Death of the Virgin* and Mantegna's panel in the Prado. His evaluation was developed along different lines: A. Venturi could never quite decide whether to attribute the drawing for the mosaic to Castagno or to Mantegna (or at least to an artist connected with the Paduan school): Fiocco strongly attributed the idea for this mosaic to Mantegna, claiming the artist was assisted by his father-in-law, Jacopo Bellini—and in fact a Jacopo is listed among the artists who were working in St Mark's when, according to Fiocco, Mantegna went to Venice. Longhi, on the other hand, has never accepted that Mantegna had anything to do with the mosaic and concluded that it was a derivation of the Prado panel.

Plate 166

CROUCHING SOLDIER. *80 × 48. Padua, Museo Civico.* Fragment from a detached fresco of a *Martyrdom of St Sebastian,* perhaps the one in the house of Dondi dell'Orologio at Padua (De Toni, *Bollettino del Museo Civico di Padua,* 1898). This work is generally excluded from the œuvre of Mantegna, although A. Venturi attributed it—if not to Mantegna himself—at least to his school.

Plate 167

THE HOLY FAMILY WITH A FE-MALE SAINT. *Canvas, 57 × 45.5. New York, Metropolitan Museum of Art.* Formerly owned by Pietro D'Aiuti, then part of the Weber Collection in Hamburg; acquired for the Altman Collection in 1913 and from there to its present location. Attributed to Mantegna by Bode (*Kunstchronik,* 1904) who dated it 1495; Woermann agreed; Knapp rejected it as an autograph work; De Ricci identified it with a canvas mentioned by Boschini in the Incurabili Hospital in Venice (*Les Arts,* 1912). Berenson and Fiocco ascribed it to Mantegna's late period. A. Venturi linked it correctly with the *Holy Family and St John the Baptist with His Family* in Mantua. The canvas therefore should be attributed, with reservations, to Francesco Mantegna.

Plate 168

THE DEAD CHRIST. *Canvas, 63.7 × 75.7. New York, Jacob M. Heimann Gallery.* Published by H. Tietze (*Art in America,* 1941) as the authentic *Foreshortened Christ* that was in Mantegna's study after his death and was later owned by Cardinal Sigismondo Gonzaga. E. Tietze-Conrat claims this to be the original model from which the other versions are derived —in which figures of mourners are inserted, such as the Brera *Dead Christ* (plate 130) and one mentioned by Summonte in Naples, now lost. The absolutely perfect resemblance between the Brera and the New York picture makes it difficult to believe that Mantegna could have copied his own work so accurately. With the exception of Fiocco (1961) the New York canvas is unanimously thought to be a copy. (See also comment on plate 130.)

Plate 169

THE ADORATION OF THE MAGI. *Canvas, 54.5 × 71. Northampton, Castle Ashby, collection of the Marquess of Northampton.* The attribution to Mantegna was grounded on the fact that, from an artistic point of view, it is the best example of a composition that has been copied over and over again. Kristeller mentions eight copies, all by artists who were in Mantegna's circle. The closest copy of this canvas is in the Johnson Collection in Philadelphia. Kristeller considered this work an early Mantegna, possibly before 1457; Knapp rejects the authenticity of the execution, Berenson includes it, without any comment, among Mantegna's late paintings; Fiocco and E. Tietze-

Conrat merely state that authenticity cannot be entirely ruled out; A. Venturi, perhaps rightly, noted a possible link with the style of Francesco Mantegna, who adhered strictly to his father's principles. In 1941 an anonymous contributor to *L'Arte* published a *Head of a Moor* (canvas, 39 × 28; Milan; Private Collection) as an autograph Mantegna. In fact this is only a copy, and an ugly one, of a figure in the Northampton composition. A copy of the *Virgin and Child* is in the Brivio Collection and has been presented to the Ambrosiana as a Mantegna.

Plate 170

MADONNA AND CHILD WITH SS JEROME AND LOUIS. *Panel, 67 × 43. Paris, Musée Jacquemart-André.* Acquired in Venice in 1887 by Guggenheim. The two saints are Jerome and Louis. The panel is thought to be a workshop production by Kristeller and he tentatively attributes it to Bonsignori; A. Venturi shares this view; Berenson listed it as a Mantegna; so did Fiocco, who dated it in the period of the Ovetari Chapel frescoes. Paccagnini considered this panel was painted by Mantegna possibly assisted by Gentile Bellini, but certainly by a member of the Bellini family; Longhi definitely assigns the execution to Giovanni Bellini; Meiss, Arslan, and Gilbert attribute it to Mantegna or to one of his followers.

Plate 171

VIRGIN AND CHILD WITH THREE SAINTS. *Canvas, 57 × 42. Paris, Musée Jacquemart-André.* From the Reiset Collection, and believed to be a detached fresco. The identity of the three saints has not been definitely established and the bad condition of the painting prevents judgment. Berenson considers it a workshop production or, alternatively, a work that has been altered by repaintings. Fiocco classifies it as a late Mantegna. Crowe and Cavalcaselle thought it may have been the *Virgin and Child* painted for Eleanor of Aragon in 1485. Apart from a few differences, this composition is a perfect reversal of the *Holy Family with a Female Saint* in Verona.

Plate 172

ECCE HOMO. *Canvas, 54 × 42. Paris, Musée Jacquemart-André.* From the antique-dealer, Bardini of Florence. The two figures on either side of Christ have been variously identified as guards or as representatives of the Synagogue or Gentiles. This work is unanimously considered a school production, but Kristeller was wrong in assigning it to Liberale da Verona. A. Venturi listed it among the works which he ascribed to Francesco Mantegna. It is a very fine painting and remarkably close to Mantegna's manner toward the end of the fifteenth century.

Plate 173

CHRIST CARRYING THE CROSS. *Canvas, 52 × 65. Verona, Museo di Castelvecchio.* Sold by Count Morando de Rizzoni to the Bernasconi Gallery. Generally accepted as a work by Francesco Mantegna. Fiocco has pointed out that this is a finer work than the similar composition in Christ Church, Oxford, which came from the collection of Charles I and is attributed to Mantegna. The condition of the painting, however, prevents any definite opinion. Berenson considers it a copy or a badly restored original. E. Tietze-Conrat links it with the *Christ Seated on a Sarcophagus* in Copenhagen (plate 141), but does not comment on its authenticity. Paccagnini attributes it to Francesco Mantegna.

Plate 174

DAVID WITH THE HEAD OF GOLIATH. *Canvas, 48.5 × 36.5. Vienna, Kunsthistorisches Museum.* Recorded in the Gonzaga Library in Mantua in 1627, and believed to have passed, after that date, into the possession of Charles I and later of the Archduke Leopold Wilhelm. Together with the *Sacrifice of Abraham* (plate 175)—it has the same dimensions—it was to have formed part of the London series of *Samson and Delilah* (plate 147). Accepted as an autograph by Kristeller, but generally attributed to Mantegna's school.

Plate 175

THE SACRIFICE OF ABRAHAM. *Canvas, 48.5 × 36.5. Vienna, Kunsthistorisches Museum.* (See comment on previous plate.)

Plate 176

ST JEROME. *Panel, 76 × 53. Washington, D.C., National Gallery of Art (Mellon Collection).* Published by A. Venturi (*L'Arte*, 1927) as an autograph work by Mantegna. Fiocco accepted the attribution and assigned the panel to the Eremitani period. Mantegna's authorship is rejected by Longhi and E. Tietze-Conrat; the latter critic sees here the mannerism of a Ferrarese artist influenced by Squarcione.

Of the numerous other works attributed to Mantegna in old catalogues—P. Kristeller has provided an almost complete list of these —I should like to mention, but not publish because of lack of sufficient evidence, the following:

Part of the illuminated initials on a book by Strabo presented by Jacopo Antonio Marcello to René of Anjou in 1459. Meiss assumed this work to be the *operetta* that prevented Mantegna from leaving Padua for Mantua when expected, *Albi* (*France*), *Bibliothèque Rochegude* (Manuscript No. 4).

THE RESURRECTION (workshop production, perhaps Francesco Mantegna). *Bergamo, Accademia Carrara.* Portrait of Gianfrancesco Gonzaga (initialled A.A. and ascribed to Bonsignori before Longhi attributed it to Gentile Bellini). *Bergamo, Accademia Carrara.*

SS JEROME AND ALEXIS (assigned by Morelli and Frizzoni to Giorgio Schiavone and by A. Venturi to Marco Zoppo). *Bergamo, Accademia Carrara.*

PIETÀ (a miniature, and a poor imitation of a drawing by Andrea). *Cleveland, Ohio, Museum of Arts.* (See plate 177*.)

PORTRAIT OF ELISABETTA GONZAGA (attributed by Crowe and Cavalcaselle to Bonsignori, by Morelli to Caroto and by Knapp to Costa). *Florence, Uffizi.*

THE RESURRECTION (generally attributed to the School but ascribed by Fiocco to Crivelli). *London, National Gallery.* (See plate 178*.)

THE THREE MARYS AT THE SEPULCHER (same attributions and location as the above). (See plate 179*.)

NOLI ME TANGERE (same attributions and location as the above). (See plate 180*.)

ENTHRONED VIRGIN AND CHILD (falsely inscribed ANDREA MANTINEA P.P. 1461; correctly attributed by Kristeller to Butinone). *Milan, Gallarati Scotti Collection.*

* These plates are reproduced only for the reader's interest. Ed. note.

MUCIUS SCAEVOLA (a mono-chrome, reduced on the left side. Fiocco considers it to have been painted by Mantegna assisted by others; Berenson considers it a late original; the attribution was rejected by Kristeller; E. Tietze-Conrat is right in assigning it to a Venetian imitator; Paccagnini describes it as a workshop production; Gilbert believes it a copy). *Munich, Graphische Sammlung*.

PORTRAIT OF FRANCESCO GONZAGA (?) (a miniature attributed to Mantegna by Berenson; the authorship is rejected by Fiocco and also by E. Tietze-Conrat who believes it is a Venetian derivation from an original). *New York, Metropolitan Museum of Art*. (See plate 181*.)

THE CRUCIFIXION (in poor condition. Attributed by Berenson to Jacopo da Montagnana; by Bode to Bramantino; by Suida to Mantegna; E. Tietze-Conrat believes it is an interesting imitation of the master's early style by a late fifteenth-century artist. (In fact the links with Mantegna are negligible.) *New York, Historical Society*. (See plate 182.*)

THE JUDGMENT OF SOLOMON (one of the series of monochromes of the same dimensions, the finest of which is the *Samson and Delilah* in London. Berenson, Fiocco and E. Tietze-Conrat assigned it to Mantegna's workshop; but E. Tietze-Conrat thinks Mantegna may have designed it; Paccagnini accepts most of it as an original). *Paris, Louvre*.

Part of the illuminated manuscript of the Life of *St Marcellus* presented by Jacopo Antonio Marcello to René of Anjou in 1453; the attribution is by Meiss. *Paris, Bibliothèque de l'Arsenal* (Manuscript No. 940).

THE HOLY FAMILY. (Mural frieze, attributed to Mantegna only by Hermanin.) *Recanati, Cathedral*.

SPHINXES, FLOWERING BRANCHES, CHERUBS AND SAINTS. *Rome, Palazzo Venezia, Sala del Mappamondo*.

FEMALE SAINT (OR VIRGIN) PRAYING (attributed to Mantegna by Suida and Fiocco; E. Tietze-Conrat assigns it to Antonio da Pavia, accepting the original signature *Ant. Papien.*, amended by a restorer to read *Andreas Pat.*, the background is copied from the *St George* in Venice). *San Diego, California, Fine Arts Museum*. (See plate 183*.)

A GROUP OF SINGERS (lunette, attributed to Mantegna by Cecchelli; Fiocco assigns it to the circle of Melozzo and Palmezzano). *Vatican City (Rome), Palace of Innocent VIII, Belvedere*.

VIRGIN AND SLEEPING CHILD (attributed to Mantegna by L. Venturi who dated it some time before the *San Zeno Altarpiece;* ascribed by E. Tietze-Conrat to a Venetian pupil; Paccagnini, stressing the fact that the painting is in too bad a condition for definite judgment, wavers between Mantegna and Marco Zoppo; Longhi (1962) calls it a weak derivation from a motif by Mantegna. The findings concerning this work and its history have been collected by Gonzales Palacios in *Paragone*, 1961, No. 143). *Formerly in the Gualino Collection, and now in Turin, Galleria Sabauda*.

DECORATIVE FRIEZE (considered by Fiocco as evidence of Mantegna's visit to Venice in 1456–7; Longhi and E. Tietze-Conrat, attribute it to a late and mediocre pupil). *Venice, Church of Santa Maria Gloriosa dei Frari, Cornaro Tomb.*

VIRGIN AND CHILD WITH ST JULIANA (listed by Berenson as a copy; Fiocco attributes it to a follower from Verona; it is in fact a mediocre workshop painting). *Verona, Museo di Castelvecchio.*

PORTRAIT OF FRANCESCO SFORZA (signed: AN. MANTINIA PINXIT ANNO MCCCCLV; perhaps a copy by Bonsignori of an original

which, however, must have been painted later than the date in the inscription). *Washington, D.C., National Gallery of Art.*

MADONNA AND CHILD (attributed by Monod to the School of Mantegna; C. Ricci was very perceptive in ascribing it to Correggio. His opinion was shared by Longhi, Perkins, and, at first, Suida (1938); Fiocco considers it a late Mantegna, and is supported by Berenson, Richter, and, in 1940, by Suida; E. Tietze-Conrat rejects both attributions). *Washington, D.C., National Gallery of Art.* (See plate 184*.)

LOCATION OF PAINTINGS

ASOLO (formerly)
VALIER COLLECTION
Christ Descending into Hell (plate 154; attribution).

BASEL
PRIVATE COLLECTION
Madonna and Child (plate 156; attribution).

BERGAMO
ACCADEMIA CARRARA
Madonna and Child (plate 138).

BERLIN
STAATLICHES MUSEEN
The Presentation in the Temple (plate 66).
Madonna with Sleeping Child (plate 69).
Portrait of Cardinal Lodovico Mezzarota (plate 67).
Virgin and Child with Cherubim (plate 157; attribution).

BOSTON
(MASSACHUSETTS)
ISABELLA STEWART GARDNER MUSEUM
Sacra Conversazione (plate 155; attribution).

MUSEUM OF FINE ARTS
Madonna and Child (plate 158b; attribution).

CINCINNATI (OHIO)
ART MUSEUM
Tarquinius and the Sibyl (plate 112).

COPENHAGEN
STATENS MUSEUM FOR KUNST
Christ Seated on a Sarcophagus and Supported by Two Angeis (plate 141).

CORREGGIO
CONGREGAZIONE DI CARITA
The Savior (plate 127).

DRESDEN
GEMÄLDEGALERIE
Madonna and Child with the Infant St John and Saints (plate 139).

DUBLIN
NATIONAL GALLERY OF IRELAND
Judith (plate 160; attribution).

FERRARA
VENDEGHINI COLLECTION
Christ with the Animula of the Virgin (plate 75).

FLORENCE
UFFIZI
The Florence Triptych (plates 70–76).

Portrait of Cardinal Carlo de' Medici (plate 78).
The Madonna of the Stonecutters (plates 122–125).

FRANKFURT-AM-MAIN
STAEDELSCHES KUNSTINS-TITUT
St Mark (plate 162; attribution).

HAMPTON COURT
The Triumphs of Caesar (plates 113–121).

INVERGARRY (SCOTLAND)
WILLIAM U. GOODBODY COLLECTION
Madonna and Child (plate 158a; attribution).

LONDON
NATIONAL GALLERY
The Agony in the Garden (plates 45–47).
Virgin and Child with St John the Baptist and Mary Magdalen (plate 134).
The Holy Family with St John (The Infant Christ as Ruler of the World) (plate 140).
The Triumph of Scipio (plates 144, 145).
The Vestal Virgin Tuccia with a Sieve (plate 146a).
Sophonisba (plate 146b).
Samson and Delilah (plate 147).
The Resurrection (plate 178; attribution).
The Three Marys at the Sepulcher (plate 179; attribution).
Noli the Tangere (plate 180; attribution).

MADRID
PRADO
The Death of the Virgin (plates 76 and 77).

MANTUA
PALAZZO DUCALE
Mural Decorations in the Camera degli Sposi (plates 80–107).

CHURCH OF SANT' ANDREA
The Holy Family with St John the Baptist and His Parents (plate 159; attribution).

MUSEO DEL PALAZZO DUCALE
Occasio and Paenitentia (plate 161; attribution).

MILAN
BRERA GALLERY
The St Luke Polyptych (plates 13–21).
Virgin and Child with Cherubim (plate 128).
The Dead Christ (plates 130 and 131).
St Bernardino (plate 164; attribution).

CIVICO MUSEO DEL CASTELLO SFORZESCO
Madonna and Child with Four Saints (plates 135–137).

POLDI PEZZOLI MUSEUM
Virgin and Child (plate 126).
Portrait of a Gentleman (plate 163; attribution).

MONTREAL
ART ASSOCIATION
Judith (plate 148).
Dido (plate 149).

NAPLES

Museo Nazionale di Capodimonte

St Euphemia (plate 32).
Portrait of Cardinal Francesco Gonzaga (plate 68).

NEW YORK

Metropolitan Museum of Art

Madonna and Child with Cherubim (plate 31).
The Adoration of the Shepherds (plate 44).
The Holy Family with a Female Saint (plate 167; attribution).

Jacob M. Heimann Gallery

The Dead Christ (plate 168; attribution).

NORTHAMPTON CASTLE ASHBY

Collection of the Marquess of Northampton

The Adoration of the Magi (plate 169; attribution).

PADUA

Church of the Eremitani

Frescoes in the Ovetari Chapel (plates 1–11, 22–29, 33–43).

Museo Antoniano

SS Anthony and Bernardino Holding the Monogram of Christ in a Wreath (plate 12).

Museo Civico

Crouching Soldier (plate 166; attribution).

PARIS

Louvre

The Crucifixion (plate 57).
St Sebastian (plates 109–111).
Madonna della Vittoria (plates 132, 133).
Parnassus (plate 150).
The Triumph of Virtue (plate 151).
Comus, the God of Revelry (plates 152 and 153).

Musée Jacquemart-André

Madonna and Child with SS Jerome and Louis (plate 170; attribution).
Virgin and Child with Three Saints (plate 171; attribution).
Ecce Homo (plate 172; attribution).

SÃO PAULO (BRAZIL)

Art Museum

St Jerome in the Wilderness (plate 65).

TURIN

Galleria Sabauda

Madonna and Child with the Infant St John and Saints (plate 129).

TOURS

Museum

The Agony in the Garden (plate 56).
The Resurrection (plate 58).

VENICE

Gallerie dell' Accademia

St George (plates 60 and 62).

CA' D'ORO
St Sebastian (plate 142).

BASILICA DI SAN MARCO
The Death of the Virgin (plate 165; attribution).

VERONA

BASILICA OF SAN ZENO MAGGIORE
The San Zeno Altarpiece (plates 48–55).

MUSEO DI CASTELVECCHIO
The Holy Family with a Female Saint (plate 143).
Christ Carrying the Cross (plate 173; attribution).

VIENNA

KUNSTHISTORISCHES MUSEUM
St Sebastian (plates 61, 63, and 64).
David with the Head of Goliath (plate 174; attribution).
The Sacrifice of Abraham (plate 175; attribution).

WASHINGTON, D.C.

NATIONAL GALLERY OF ART
The Christ Child Standing in a Niche (plate 30).
Portrait of a Gentleman (plate 79).
Judith (plate 108).
St Jerome (plate 176; attribution).
Madonna and Child (plate 184; attribution).

SELECTED CRITICISM

No man who ever took up or used a brush or any other instrument of art was as worthy as he (Mantegna) of being called the true successor of the ancient masters, for none painted more beautifully. Indeed, if it is not too much to say, the beauty that he created was greater than theirs, and I place him before them.

His diligent and admirable use of colors, his knowledge of the rules of perspective, his draftsmanship would astound anyone who looks at his foreshortened pictures that delude the eye and cause all art to rejoice.

GIOVANNI SANTI.
Cronaca rimata, 1482–94,

Michelangelo replied: ". . . No less noble is the palace of the Dukes of Mantua, where Andrea (Mantegna) painted the Triumph of Caius Caesar. And even more remarkable are the stables decorated by Giulio (Romano), Raphael's pupil, who is flourishing in Mantua nowadays. . . ."

FRANCISCO DE HOLLANDA
La pittura antica, 1538.

. . . he displayed much judgment and forethought in this work (*The Triumphs of Caesar*) for the plane on which the figures stand is above eye-level so that the figures in the foreground stand on the first line of the plane, and those in the back recede so that their feet and legs are lost to view in the exact proportions required. And in the same manner he treated the spoils, vases and other accessories and ornaments, of which he permitted only the lower part to be seen, the upper part being lost to view, as required by the rules of perspective. . . . We perceive, then, that these excellent masters carefully examined the different properties of natural objects and imitated them with studious care.

GIORGIO VASARI,
Lives of the Artists, second edition 1568.

Mantegna was the first to open our eyes to this art (perspective), for he understood that without it, the art of painting is indeed nothing. He has taught us, therefore, how to make everything correspond to man's way of seeing things, and this one may see in his most diligently executed works.

GIAN PAOLO LOMAZZO,
Idea del Tempio della Pittura, 1590.

Andrea deserved to be celebrated by Ariosto no less for the gentleness of his ways then for the excellence of his painting. Ariosto included him among the most famous artists of his time in the following line:

"Leonardo, Andrea Mantegna, Gian Bellino . . ." (canto XXXIII).

FILIPPO BALDINUCCI,
Notizie de' professori del disegno, etc., 1681.

In the Church of the Eremitani I saw some astonishing paintings by Mantegna, one of the old masters. What a sharp, assured actuality they have! It was from this actuality, which does not merely appeal to the imagination, but is solid, lucid, scrupulously exact and has something austere, even laborious about it, that the later painters drew their strength, as I observed in Titian's pictures. It was thanks to this that their genius and energy were able to rise above the earth and create heavenly forms which are still real. It was thus that art developed after the Dark Ages.

JOHANN WOLFGANG GOETHE,
Italian Journey, 1786. (W. H. Auden and Elisabeth Mayer translation.)

It is wonderful to see (in the *Madonna della Vittoria*) such delicate complexions, such shining armor, such iridescent robes, and the fresh and dewy ornamental fruit. Each head is a study in liveliness and character, and some of them should teach us how to imitate antiquity. The whole composition, in its nude as well as its clothed figures, has a mellowness that completely negates the common opinion which says that "in the style of Mantegna" means "in the dryest of all styles." The blending of colors, the subtlety of the brushwork, the extraordinary grace of this painting are such that I would call it the final step in art before Leonardo's achievement of perfection.

LUIGI LANZI,
Storia pittorica dell' Italia, 1796.

There are three distinct qualities conspicuous in the subject of St James performing the rite of baptism, which are not always found united in Mantegna. In a very earnest spirit and with studied thought he seeks to combine the stately composure of statuary, the momentary action of nature, and an excessive simplicity of realism.

Mantegna from the first betrays a total absence of that feeling for tone which is so charming in Giovanni Bellini. He contrasts his tints on scientific principles, one color being accurately balanced by another, in accordance with the laws of harmony; but he has not the fibre of a colorist, nor does he know how to produce depth by imperceptible gradations; and in his merciless severity he is the forerunner of Carpaccio, the Signorelli of the North.

CROWE and CAVALCASELLE,
A History of Painting in North Italy, 1871.

Mantegna deserves no blame for Romanizing Christianity, any more than Raphael for Hellenizing Hebraism. Indeed, they both did their work so well that the majority of Europeans at this day still visualize their Bible story in forms derived from these two Renaissance masters. And Mantegna should incur the less reproach because it is probable that the Christian spirit cannot easily find embodiment in the visual arts. The purpose of the last few paragraphs was not to find fault with Mantegna but to show that, as an illustrator, he intended to be wholly Roman. Had he succeeded, we might perhaps afford to forget him, in spite of the three centuries of admiration bestowed upon him by an over-Latinized Europe. We do not any longer need his reconstructions. We know almost scientifically the aspect and character of the Rome which cast her glamor over his fancy. Besides, we no longer stop at Rome, but have gone back to her fountain-head, Athens. If Mantegna is still inspiring as an illustrator, it is because he failed of his object, and conveyed, instead of an archaeologically correct transcript of ancient Rome, a creation of his own romantic mood, the Rome of his dreams, his vision of a noble humanity living nobly in noble surroundings.

BERNARD BERENSON,
The Italian Painters of the Renaissance, 1897 (1952 edition).

To the genial painter there could be no lack of ever new and profound forms of expression, even in religious pictures. But in his innermost feelings he must have grown more and more estranged from the religious spirit of Christianity the more unreservedly his enthusiasm waxed for antiquity, and the more not only his mind, but also his sense-perception, was taken up with the shapes of the ancient world, as it appeared to him. If in his early works he came near—may one say?—to the Aeschylean spirit, in the later works there breaks through, even more strongly, the Euripidean apprehension of the tragic, the sympathy with the human will as against all-determining fate.

PAUL KRISTELLER,
Andrea Mantegna, 1902.

Mantegna's draftsmanship is constantly large, lucid, pure, noble, and supremely erudite. Not for him the comfortable temptation of soft, blended contours, the easy refinement of half-tints. He is for ever translating his thoughts as an artist with incisive accuracy and daring. There is no uncertainty or effort about his lines: they are deep and genuine. He does not worry in the least about appearing too dry or too hard.

L. TESTI,
La storia della pittura veneziana, 1909.

The founder of North Italian Humanistic painting began working filled with enthusiasm for antiquity. He used antiquity to Romanize Donatello's forms, and he simplified their composition and reduced their movement. Unscrupulous naturalist that he was, he went on trying to enlarge nature, to strengthen it, so that it could withstand the proximity of his magnificent ancient images. Mantegna's iconography, therefore, consists in the first place of an iron-like gravity, of deep silence, of a feeling of *Imperium*. . . .

In Mantua the practiced master had to prove himself equal to two tasks, for he was expected to compete with the detail of the enamel-like Northern painters, and to produce a faithful portrayal of the Gonzaga court. In the first instance, he overcame all difficulties: he added color to his Biblical bas-reliefs, he even painted a cherub in the Byzantine fashion, as if he were reproducing ancient gilded bronzes. He reduced the old monumental environments to the size of cameos and he carried figures and compositions to the point of improbability. In the second instance, the naturalist stood aside from the lover of antiquity: the naturalist pursued reality far into the worlds of ugliness and ridicule; the lover of antiquity opposed to this his Caesarean pride. Only when Mantegna came to the open vaulting did he abandon his study of human skin and whiteness of marble, and then his genius soared high above the little world that the artist had so imposingly arranged. . . .

ADOLFO VENTURI,
Storia dell' Arte Italiana, VII, 3, 1914.

But so far as Mantegna is concerned, we cannot see his origins other than in Padua, and in that special and unrealistic transformation that occurred there about 1450 because of that strange Florentine spirit that constituted Donatello's gold, copper, and ivory altar in the Church of the Santo.

Fantastic though it may seem, we are deeply convinced that everything that was exchanged between Padua, Ferrara and Venice from 1450 to 1470—from the wild follies of Tura and

Crivelli to the sorrowful elegance of young Bellini, and eventually to the apparently severe principles established by Mantegna—had its origin in that undisciplined band of wanderers, the sons of tailors, barbers, cobblers, and peasants, who during those twenty years passed through Squarcione's studio. The studio itself must have been undescribable. Only an artist like De Chirico could conceive it: a dusky, menacing atmosphere, in which the decapitated busts of classical statues supported the twisted frames waiting for triptychs commissioned by the Bishops of Polesine; Florentine plaquettes being used as palettes for Prussian blue; Chinese carpets depicting glaring monsters heaped with moth-eaten rolls of cloth tossed there by Squarcione, *sartus et recamator* . . . here and there, a terrible yellow dust settling down on the milk-white plaster-casts, and, all day long, the noisy comings-and-goings of Donatello's joking assistants.

It was amid all this Mantegna grew up. . . .

ROBERTO LONGHI,
"Lettera pittorica", etc., in Vita artistica, 1926.

The young artist was undoubtedly a most sincere admirer of the classical past, and indeed he was undoubtedly more conscious than anyone else of antiquity. Helped from the beginning by the equally enthusiastic recollections of his father-in-law, Jacopo Bellini, he transformed antiquity into a reality as worthy as antiquity itself had been. I mean to say, that no one understood antiquity better than he, and when he found it convenient to evoke it, he translated it into a style that, naive though it may appear to the archaeologist, none the less possesses all the peculiarities and indeed the aspects of antiquity, because that was the aspect of Mantegna's own art. The antiquity which he constantly and ardently questioned, is brought back to life in forms which have all the flavor, dignity and rhythm of the original era. And the same might be said of a Shakespeare tragedy that evokes Julius Caesar.

Certainly Mantegna interpreted it as no one else could ever do, because there was a correspondence between the detachment of those things which, though still extant and needing nothing other than their eternal expression, are still classical, and his preference for lofty, serene and, in their own way, disinterested experiences—not to speak of the divine indifference of Piero della Francesca. Mantegna's lofty world is marked by intimate and potential labor; it is a world that does not like wasting itself in gesture and emphasis which is unnecessary for the olympic self-control that comes from perfect poise. It was his followers who were guilty of confusing classicism with Renaissance.

GIUSEPPE FIOCCO,
Mantegna—La cappella Ovetari.

I recall that Lanzi, more than a hundred and fifty years ago, said of Mantegna that he not only adopted "that care for detail that can easily degenerate into dryness," but that he "neglected the element capable of animating dead images, and which we call expression." Fortunately this was not always the case for Mantegna, and this, I believe, was due to his early link with his brother-in-law, Giovanni Bellini. If Mantegna indeed made an effort to "animate dead images" until approximately 1455 and—starting with the major panels of the *San Zeno Altarpiece* (1456–59)—decided to give up sentiment altogether, it is clear that he was influenced in this by Giovanni Bellini, who could only witness in silence the noble though obsessive archaeological fixation of his friend and brother-in-law. We would be eternally grateful to anyone who could reconstruct the lively conversations that must have occurred between the two young artists, more often than not on the barge carrying them from Venice to Padua and back again to Venice.

Perhaps they met again after 1460 to discuss their very similar interpretations of the *Presentation in the Temple*. . . . But after this the conversation was interrupted for ever.

A *St Sebastian* such as Bellini's in San Zanipolo has nothing left in common with the one that Mantegna was to paint later in Mantua. It is probable that by then Mantegna had already visited Tuscany, and it is surprising to find no evidence of his having thought about the great Tuscan naturalists of forty, thirty, twenty years earlier. Leaving aside Arezzo (Piero della Francesca), whom some would see a reflection of in the *Camera degli Sposi*, we ask ourselves whether the artist had even bothered to look at the Carmine frescoes (Masaccio). The fact that, a year later, he refused to work in the Camposanto in Pisa makes one wonder whether it was not he who, being asked for advice, suggested the name of Benozzo Gozzoli. All this is possible, if it is true that the only Tuscan echo in the *Camera degli Sposi* derives—for what it is worth—from the chapel of the Medici Palace, decorated (by Gozzoli) a few years earlier. Therefore, when Mantegna came to paint the *Camera*, he found that the real meaning of that vast mural solution was a closed door to him (he dealt with the most difficult parts by applying the "panel" technique). Even the *trompe l'oeil* experiment in the ceiling, so admired as a precedent to Correggio (which thematically it is not), is ultimately to be considered a signal failure.

ROBERTO LONGHI,
"Crivelli e Mantegna: due mostre interferenti," etc., in Paragone, 1962.

BIBLIOGRAPHICAL NOTE

For fuller bibliographical information on Mantegna the reader is referred to Paul Kristeller's *Andrea Mantegna* (Berlin and Leipzig, 1902) and Giuseppe Fiocco's *Mantegna* (Milan, 1937). The author limits himself to listing here only those sources fundamental for a study of Mantegna, together with recent contributions.

M. A. MICHIEL. *Notizie d'opere del disegno,* 1525–43 (Frizzoni: Bologna 1884).

G. VASARI. *Le Vita,* Florence 1550; second edition, Florence 1568.

B. SCARDEONE. *De antiquitati urbis Patavii,* Basel 1560.

D. BARBARO. *La practica della perspettiva,* Venice 1568.

G. P. LOMAZZO. *Idea del Tempio della pittura,* Milan 1590.

C. RIDOLFI. *Le meraviglie dell'arte,* Venice 1648 (Hadeln: Berlin 1914).

G. P. CHATTARD. *Nuova descrizione del Vaticano,* Rome 1762–67.

P. BRANDOLESE. *Pitture, sculture ed altre cose notabili di Padova,* Padua 1795, pp. 216 ff.

G. A. MOSCHINI. *Delle origini e delle vicende della pittura in Padova,* Venice 1826.

C. D'ARCO. *Delle arti e degli artefici di Mantova,* Mantua 1857.

G. CAMPORI. *Raccolta di cataloghi ed inventari inediti,* Modena 1870.

J. A. CROWE and G. B. CAVALCASELLE. *A History of Painting in North Italy,* London 1871.

H. THODE. *Andrea Mantegna,* Bielefeld-Leipzig 1897.

C. YRIARTE. *Andrea Mantegna,* Paris 1901.

P. KRISTELLER. *Andrea Mantegna,* London 1901; Berlin and Leipzig 1902.

M. CRUTWELL. *Mantegna,* London 1908.

L. TESTI. *La storia della pittura veneziana,* Bergamo 1909–25.

P. KRISTELLER. "F. Squarcione e le sue relazioni con A. Mantegna," in *Rassegna d'arte,* 1909.

F. KNAPP. *Andrea Mantegna,* Stuttgart and Leipzig 1910.

A. VENTURI. *Storia dell'arte italiana,* VII, 3; Milan 1914.

E. PANOFSKY. "Perspective als symbolische Form," in *Vorräge der Bibliothek Warburg,* 1924–25. Leipzig 1927.

G. FIOCCO. *L'arte di Andrea Mantegna,* Bologna 1926.

R. LONGHI. "Lettera pittorica a Giuseppe Fiocco su 'L'arte del Mantegna'," in *Vita artistica,* November 1926 (Fiocco's reply is in the same issue, and Longhi's reply to this is in the December issue).

E. RIGONI. "Nuovi documenti sul Mantegna," in *Atti del R. Istitute veneto di scienze, lettere ed arti,* 1927–28.

G. FIOCCO. "Andrea Mantegna," in Thieme-Becker, *Künstler-Lexicon,* Leipzig 1930.

R. LONGHI. "Risarcimento di un Mantegna," in *Pan,* 1930.

G. FIOCCO. *Mantegna,* Milan 1937.

C. L. RAGGHIANTI. "Casa Vitaliani," in *Critica d'arte,* 1937.

G. FIOCCO. Various essays in *Bollettino del Museo Civico di Padova*. 1939–40.

A. LUZIO and R. PARIBENI. *Il trionfo di Cesare di Andrea Mantegna*, Rome 1940.

H. TIETZE. "The *Dead Christ* by Mantegna," in *Art in America*, 1941.

H. TIETZE. "Mantegna and his companions in Squarcione's workshop," in *Art in America*, 1942.

H. TIETZE and E. TIETZE-CONRAT. "What Degas Learned from Mantegna," in *Gazette des Beaux-Arts*, 1945.

F. FORLATI and M. L. GENGARO. *La chiesa degli Eremitani a Padova*, Florence 1945.

V. MOSCHINI. *Gli affreschi del Mantegna agli Eremitani di Padova*, Bergamo 1946.

G. FIOCCO. *Mantegna*, Milan 1946.

W. E. SUIDA. "Mantegna und Melozzo," in *Art in America*, 1946.

H. TIETZE and E. TIETZE-CONRAT. "Mantegna's Parnassus. A Discussion of a Recent Interpretation," in *Art Bulletin*, 1949.

R. H. WILENSKI. *Mantegna and the Paduan School*, London 1949.

E. WIND. "Mantegna's Parnassus. A Reply to Some Recent Reflections," in *Art Bulletin*, 1949.

L. VERTOVA. *Mantegna*, Florence 1950.

M. DAVIES. *The Earlier Italian School, National Gallery Catalogue*, London 1951. A second edition of the National Gallery *Earlier Italian Schools* (Martin Davies) appeared in 1961.

H. TIETZE and E. TIETZE-CONRAT. *Notes on Hercules at the Crossends*, Warburg 1951.

B. BERENSON, *The Italian Painters of the Renaissance*, London 1952; first edition, London–New York 1897.

F. HARTT. "Mantegna's *Madonna of the Rocks*," in *Gazette des Beaux-Arts*, 1952.

T. TIETZE-CONRAT. *Mantegna*, London 1955.

G. ROBERTSON. "Andrea Mantegna," in *The Burlington Magazine*, 1956, p. 459.

A. BOVERO. "Ferrarese Miniatures at Turin," in *The Burlington Magazine*, 1957, pp. 261 ff.

MILLARD MEISS. *Andrea Mantegna as Illuminator*, New York 1957 (see also G. Fiocco's review in *Paragone*, March 1958).

G. PACCAGNINI. *La Camera degli Sposi*, Milan 1957.

A. MEZZETTI. "Un Ercole e Anteo del Mantegna," in *Bollettino d'Arte*, 1958, pp. 232 ff.

L. COLETTI. *La Camera degli Sposi*, with an appendix by E. Camesasca, Milan 1959.

G. PACCHIONI. *Le Camera Picta da Andrea Mantegna nel Castello di Mantova*, Milan 1959.

L. COLETTI. *La Camera Degli Sposi di Andrea Mantegna*. With appendix by E. Camesasca, Milan 1959.

G. FIOCCO. *L'arte di Andrea Mantegna*, Venice 1959.

G. PACCAGNINI. *Andrea Mantegna*, Catalog of the exhibition held at the Ducal Palace, Venice in 1961.

G. PACCAGNINI. "Appunta sulla tecnica della 'Camera picta' di Andrea Mantegna," in *Studi in onore di Mario Salmi*, Rome 1961.

G. PACCAGNINI and A. MEZZETTI. *Andrea Mantegna* (Catalogue of the Exhibition at Mantua), Venice 1961.

G. FIOCCO. *Pitture del Mantegna*, Milan 1961 (English edition, London and New York 1963).

E. ARSLAN. "Il Mantegna a Mantova," in *Commentari*, 1961, pp. 163 ff.

R. LONGHI. "Crivelli e Mantegna," in *Paragone*, January 1962.

M. SALMI and G. PACCAGNINI. *Andrea Mantegna*, Milan 1962.

C. GILBERT. "The Exhibition of Andrea Mantegna," in *The Burlington Magazine*, January 1962.

E. L. PRASS. *The Engravings of Andrea Mantegna* (*Bulletin* of the Cleveland Museum of Art, 1956).

G. FIOCCO. *Mantegna—La Cappella Ovetari Nella Chiesa Degli Eremitani*, Milan 1957, London 1963.

REPRODUCTIONS

ACKNOWLEDGEMENT FOR PLATES

Alinari, Florence: plates 9, 18, 19, 52–55, 57, 59, 109–11, 122, 123, 129, 132, 139, 150, 151. *Anderson, Florence*: plates 1–8, 10–13, 16, 20–29, 32–43, 47–51, 60, 62, 68, 70–74, 76–78, 126, 128, 130, 131, 134–8, 142, 147, 159, 164–6. *Berlin, Staatliches Museen*: plates 66, 67, 69, 157. *Boston, Isabella Stewart Gardner Museum*: plate 155. *Boston, Museum of Fine Arts*: plate 158b. *Bulloz, Paris*: plates 56, 58, 152, 153, 170–2. *Bruckmann, Munich*: plate 162. *Cincinnati (Ohio), Art Museum*: plate 112. *Copenhagen, Statens Museum for Kunst*: plate 141. *Dublin, National Gallery of Ireland*: plate 160. *Fiorentini, Venice*: plate 143. *Florence, Uffizi*: plates 124, 125. *Graphic Art Color*: plates 14, 15, 17. *Istituto Grafico Bertieri, Milan*: plates 80–107 and color plate V. *London, National Gallery*: plates 46, 113–21, 140, 144–6. *Manzotti, Correggio*: plate 127. *Milan, Poldi Pezzoli Museum*: plate 163. *Montreal, Museum of Fine Arts*: plates 148, 149. *New York, Metropolitan Museum of Art*: plates 31, 34, 167. *Perotti, Milan*: plate 65. *Scala, Florence*: color plates VII, VIII. *Vienna, Kunsthistorisches Museum*: plates 61, 63, 64, 174, 175. *Washington, D.C., National Gallery of Art*: plates 30, 79, 108, 176.

Plate 169 *is reproduced by courtesy of the Marquess of Northampton. Plates 75, 154, 156, 158a, 161, 168, 173 were obtained from private sources.*

Plate 80. THE CAMERA DEGLI SPOSI:
left wall. Mantua, Palazzo Ducale

Plate 81. THE CAMERA DEGLI SPOSI:
right wall

Plate 82. *Detail of plate 81*

Plate 83. *Detail of plate 82*

Plate 84. *Detail of plate 82*

Plate 85. *Detail of plate 82*

Plate 86. *Detail of plate 82*

Plate 87. *Detail of plate 82*

Plate 88. *Third section of plate 80*

Plate 89. *Detail of plate 88*

Plate 90. *Detail of plate 88*

Plate 91. *Detail of plate 88*

Plate 92. *Detail of plate 88*

THE CAMERA DEGLI SPOSI:
right wall. Mantua, Palazzo Ducale
(*detail of plate 81*)

Plate 93. *Detail of plate 88*

Plate 94. *Second section of plate 80, upper part*

Plate 95. *Second section of plate 80, lower part*

Plate 96. *First section of plate 80*

Plate 97. *Detail of plate 96*

Plate 98. *Detail of plate 96*

Plate 99. THE CAMERA DEGLI SPOSI:
ceiling

Plate 100. *Center detail of plate 99*

Plate 101. *Detail of plate 100*

Plate 102. THE CAMERA DEGLI SPOSI:
detail of ceiling decoration

Plate 103. THE CAMERA DEGLI SPOSI:
detail of ceiling decoration

Plate 104. THE CAMERA DEGLI SPOSI:
details of spandrels

Plate 105. THE CAMERA DEGLI SPOSI:
details of spandrels

Plate 106. THE CAMERA DEGLI SPOSI:
details of spandrels

Plate 107. THE CAMERA DEGLI SPOSI:
details of spandrels

Plate 108. JUDITH
Washington, D.C., National Gallery of Art

THE CAMERA DEGLI SPOSI:
ceiling. Mantua, Palazzo Ducale
(*detail of plate 99*)

Plate 109. ST SEBASTIAN
Paris, Louvre

Plate 110. *Detail of plate 109*

Plate III. *Detail of plate 109*

Plate 112. TARQUINIUS AND THE SIBYL
Cincinnati, Art Museum

Plate 113. THE TRIUMPHS OF CAESAR (I)
Hampton Court

Plate 114. THE TRIUMPHS OF CAESAR (II)
Hampton Court

Plate 115. THE TRIUMPHS OF CAESAR (III)
Hampton Court

Plate 116. THE TRIUMPHS OF CAESAR (IV)
Hampton Court

Plate 117. THE TRIUMPHS OF CAESAR (V)
Hampton Court

Plate 118. THE TRIUMPHS OF CAESAR (VI)
Hampton Court

Plate 119. THE TRIUMPHS OF CAESAR (VII)
Hampton Court

Plate 120. THE TRIUMPHS OF CAESAR (VIII)
Hampton Court

Plate 121. THE TRIUMPHS OF CAESAR (IX)
Hampton Court

Plate 122. THE MADONNA OF THE STONECUTTERS
Florence, Uffizi

Plate 123. *Detail of plate 122*

Plate 124. *Detail of plate 122*

VIRGIN AND CHILD WITH CHERUBIM
Milan, Brera Gallery
(*detail of plate 128*)

Plate 125. *Detail of plate 122*

Plate 126. MADONNA AND CHILD
Milan, Poldi Pezzoli Museum

Plate 127. THE SAVIOR
Correggio, Congregazione di Carità

Plate 128. VIRGIN AND CHILD WITH CHERUBIM
Milan, Brera Gallery

Plate 129. MADONNA AND CHILD WITH THE INFANT ST JOHN AND SAINTS
Turin, Galleria Sabauda

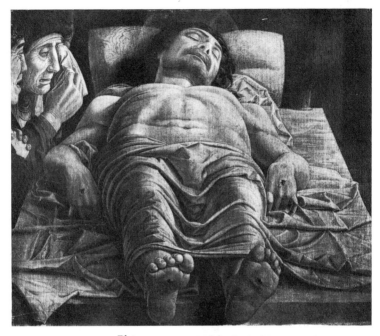

Plate 130. THE DEAD CHRIST
Milan, Brera Gallery

Plate 131. *Detail of plate 130*

Plate 132. MADONNA DELLA VITTORIA
Paris, Louvre

Plate 133. *Detail of plate 132*

Plate 134. VIRGIN AND CHILD WITH ST JOHN THE BAPTIST AND
MARY MAGDALEN
London, National Gallery

Plate 135. MADONNA AND CHILD WITH FOUR SAINTS
Milan, Civico Museo del Castello Sforzesco

Plate 136. *Detail of plate 135*

Plate 137. *Detail of plate 135*

Plate 138. MADONNA AND CHILD
Bergamo, Accademia Carrara

Plate 139. MADONNA AND CHILD WITH THE INFANT ST JOHN AND SAINTS
Dresden, Gemäldegalerie

Plate 140. THE HOLY FAMILY WITH ST JOHN
London, National Gallery

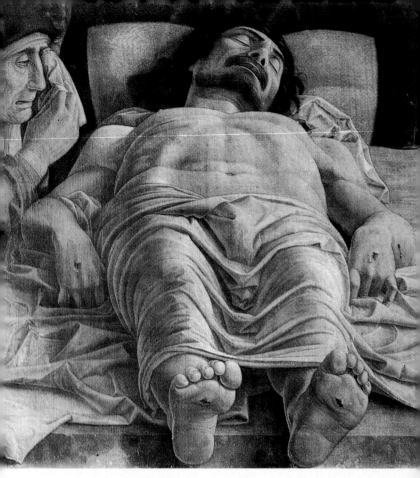

THE DEAD CHRIST
Milan, Brera Gallery
(*detail of plate 130*)

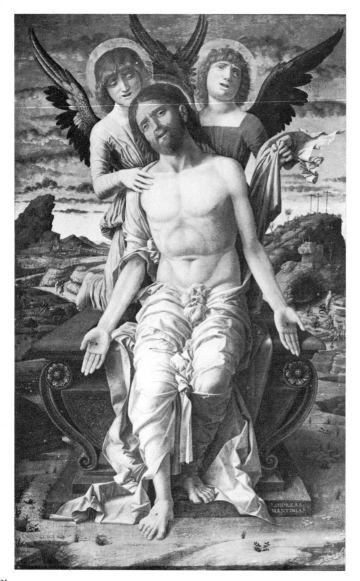

Plate 141. CHRIST SEATED ON A SARCOPHAGUS AND SUPPORTED BY
TWO ANGELS
Copenhagen, Statens Museum for Kunst

Plate 142. ST SEBASTIAN
Venice, Ca' d'Oro

Plate 143. THE HOLY FAMILY WITH A FEMALE SAINT
Verona, Museo di Castelvecchio

Plate 144. THE TRIUMPH OF SCIPIO:
left half. London, National Gallery

Plate 145. THE TRIUMPH OF SCIPIO:
right half. London, National Gallery

Plate 146. THE VESTAL VIRGIN TUCCIA WITH A SIEVE and
SOPHONISBA
London, National Gallery

Plate 147. SAMSON AND DELILAH
London, National Gallery

Plate 148. JUDITH
Montreal, Art Association

Plate 149. DIDO
Montreal, Art Association

Plate 150. PARNASSUS
Paris. Louvre

Plate 151. THE TRIUMPH OF VIRTUE
Paris, Louvre

Plate 152. COMUS, THE GOD OF REVELRY
Paris. Louvre

Plate 153. *Detail of plate 152*

Plate 154. CHRIST DESCENDING INTO HELL
formerly Asolo, Valier Collection (*attrib.*)

Plate 155. SACRA CONVERSAZIONE
Boston, Isabella Stewart Gardner Museum (*attrib.*)

Plate 156. MADONNA AND CHILD
Basel, Private Collection (*attrib.*)

Plate 157. VIRGIN AND CHILD WITH CHERUBIM
Berlin, Staatliches Museen (*attrib.*)

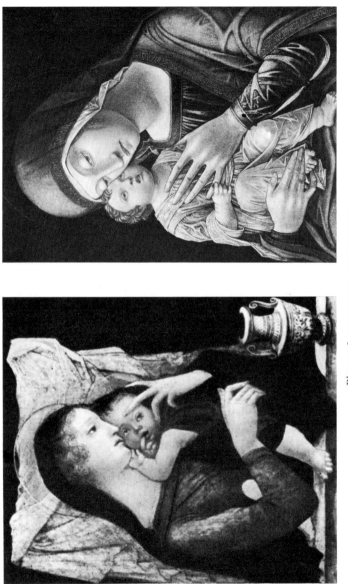

Plate 158. MADONNA AND CHILD

Invergarry, W. U. Goodbody Collection *and* Boston, Museum of Fine Arts

Plate 159. THE HOLY FAMILY WITH ST JOHN THE BAPTIST AND HIS
PARENTS
Mantua, Church of Sant'Andrea, Mantegna's Chapel (*attrib.*)

Plate 160. JUDITH
Dublin, National Gallery of Ireland (*attrib.*)

Plate 161. OCCASIO AND PAENITENTIA
Mantua, Museo del Palazzo Ducale (*attrib.*)

Plate 162. ST MARK
Frankfurt-am-Main, Staedelsches Kunstinstitut (*attrib.*)

Plate 163. PORTRAIT OF A GENTLEMAN
Milan, Poldi Pezzoli Museum (*attrib.*)

Plate 164. ST BERNARDINO
Milan, Brera Gallery (*attrib.*)

Plate 165. THE DEATH OF THE VIRGIN
Venice, Basilica di San Marco, Mascoli Chapel (*attrib.*)

Plate 166. CROUCHING SOLDIER
Padua, Museo Civico (*attrib.*)

Plate 167. THE HOLY FAMILY WITH A FEMALE SAINT
New York, Metropolitan Museum of Art (*attrib.*)

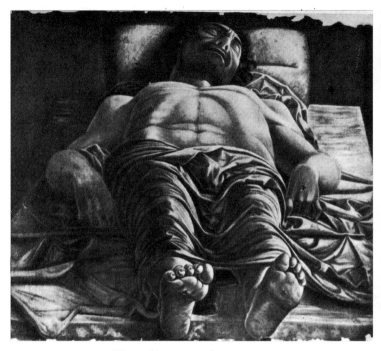

Plate 168. THE DEAD CHRIST
New York, Jacob M. Heimann Gallery (*attrib.*)

Plate 169. THE ADORATION OF THE MAGI
Northampton, Castle Ashby, collection of the Marquess of Northampton
(*attrib.*)

Plate 170. MADONNA AND CHILD WITH SS JEROME AND LOUIS
Paris, Museé Jacquemart-André (*attrib.*)

Plate 171. VIRGIN AND CHILD WITH THREE SAINTS
Paris, Museé Jacquemart-André (*attrib.*)

Plate 172. ECCE HOMO
Paris, Musée Jacquemart-André (*attrib.*)

Plate 173. CHRIST CARRYING THE CROSS
Verona, Museo di Castelvecchio (*attrib.*)

Plate 174. DAVID WITH THE HEAD OF GOLIATH
Vienna, Kunsthistorisches Museum (*attrib.*)

Plate 175. THE SACRIFICE OF ABRAHAM
Vienna, Kunsthistorisches Museum (*attrib.*)

Plate 176. ST JEROME
Washington, D.C., National Gallery of Art (*attrib.*)

Plate 177. PIETÀ
Cleveland, Ohio, Museum of Arts (*attrib.*)

Plate 178. THE RESURRECTION
London, National Gallery (*attrib.*)

Plate 179. THE THREE MARYS AT THE SEPULCHER
London, National Gallery (*attrib.*)

Plate 180. NOLI ME TANGERE
London, National Gallery (*attrib.*)

Plate 181. PORTRAIT OF FRANCESCO GONZAGA
New York, Metropolitan Museum of Art (*attrib.*)

Plate 182. THE CRUCIFIXION
New York, Historical Society (*attrib.*)

Plate 183. VIRGIN PRAYING
San Diego, California, Fine Arts Museum (*attrib.*)

Plate 184. MADONNA AND CHILD
Washington, D.C., National Gallery of Art (*attrib.*)